D0643831

ARMIES WITHOUT STATES

ARMIES WITHOUT STATES

The Privatization of Security

Robert Mandel

LYNNE
RIENNER
PUBLISHERS

BOULDER
LONDON

Published in the United States of America in 2002 by
Lynne Rienner Publishers, Inc.
1800 30th Street, Boulder, Colorado 80301
www.rienner.com

and in the United Kingdom by
Lynne Rienner Publishers, Inc.
3 Henrietta Street, Covent Garden, London WC2E 8LU

Library of Congress Cataloging-in-Publication Data
Mandel, Robert
    Armies without states : the privatization of security / Robert Mandel.
    p. cm.
    Includes bibliographical references and index.
    ISBN 1-58826-066-6 (hc : alk. paper)
    1. National security. 2. Private security services. 3. Military police.
4. Internal security. 5. Security, International. I. Title.
UA10.5 .M315   2002
327.1'7—dc21   2001059426

British Cataloguing in Publication Data
A Cataloguing in Publication record for this book
is available from the British Library.

Printed and bound in the United States of America

    5 4 3 2 1

CONTENTS

FIGURES

PREFACE

The amazing proliferation across the globe of mercenaries, private armies, militia, vigilante squads, transnational criminal organizations, self-defense forces, and survivalist enclaves in recent years has caught scholars, policymakers, and the mass public largely unprepared. Posing a basic challenge to the structure of the entire international system, with its underlying assumption that national governments should hold a virtual monopoly on instruments of coercive force, the privatization of security merits sustained analysis to describe its overall scope, delineate its many different forms, place it in a theoretical and historical context, understand its causes and consequences, and figure out how to cope with the transformation.

My desire to write this book stemmed primarily from a fascination about this coercive development. It seemed incredibly urgent to place prevailing trends in a conceptual context that would allow both understanding of and response to the developments. Notably absent from my motivations was either, on the one hand, a predetermined sense of horror at its occurrence and a desire to stamp it out, or, on the other hand, a sense of unbridled pleasure that state security authority was finally receiving a sustained challenge.

In exploring what others have written on the topic, it became increasingly clear that most people either downplay the importance or novelty of this trend, or alternatively construct arguments to prove its consummate worthiness or utter danger. Neither approach seems ultimately helpful, so instead my intent is to explore in as open-minded a manner as possible not only the broader sources and implications of security privatization but also its linkages with other changes in the post–Cold War security environment. Polemical emotional reactions to phenomena such as privatized security, based on the blinders of ignorance or ideology, are exactly what have stood in the way for so long of coherent responses to transforming defense challenges in today's world.

My thoughts in this book reflect years of pondering and constitute an extensive elaboration and significant refinement of those expressed in a journal article, "The Privatization of Security" (*Armed Forces & Society,* fall 2001). This whole topic is a logical follow-up to my two previous works dealing with global security disorder: *Deadly Transfers and the Global Playground: Transnational Security Threats in a Disorderly World* (1999); and *The Changing Face of National Security: A Conceptual Analysis* (1994). As background, I have had conversations with numerous colleagues both here and abroad in government and university settings who have significantly contributed to my thinking, and I wish to thank them collectively for their help.

Due to the recent emergence of the post–Cold War wave of privatized security, there has not been sufficient time for a vast established scholarly literature to emerge on the topic. As a result, many of the most insightful writings on the topic are still in preliminary form and unpublished. For that reason, many of the references cited in this book are from the Internet rather than from traditional books and journal and newspaper articles. While this tendency may in some way cause the credibility of some of the data to be suspect, it does not invalidate the relevance of the opinions expressed or the conceptual perspectives introduced. In particular, David Isenberg's vast electronic collection of largely unpublished pieces on the privatization of security, which he graciously shared with me, proved to be absolutely a gold mine of ideas.

However, I take full responsibility for any egregious errors found herein. With estimates of the magnitude of global privatized security revenues being very rough, with frequent rumors of unreported covert mercenary activities, and with new groups emerging all the time purporting to provide protection, the likelihood of the passage of time revealing mistakes in fact and judgment appears reasonably high. There is no question in my mind that the ideas presented in this volume will need further refinement, and one can only hope that progress occurs before global chaos ensues.

INTRODUCTION

In the post–Cold War era, the zest for privatization has spread around the world like wildfire. Associating privatization with both efficiency and effectiveness, most have hailed it as a major step forward, contrasting its benefits sharply to the failures of bloated overcentralized government bureaucracies. This unrestrained admiration for private-sector performance has caused many countries to apply this management system in virtually every conceivable sector. Most recently, even the area most tightly associated with government functioning—the provision of security for its citizenry—has fallen prey to the privatization tidal wave.

The importance of the topic was vividly highlighted in the aftermath of the terrorist attack on the United States of September 11, 2001, during which time President George W. Bush placed a sizable "wanted dead or alive" reward on key international terrorists specifically to encourage mercenaries and bounty hunters to enter Afghanistan to hunt them down, that is, to assist governments in achieving global security. For the most militarily dominant nation in the world to seek the aid of private security providers in confronting a direct threat from abroad is truly noteworthy, reinforcing both the limits on state power and the potential potency of nonstate coercion. This U.S. government act alone was sufficient to direct the attention of the entire world to a probing exploration of security privatization.

It is not an overstatement to indicate that the widespread privatization of security has the potential to send shock waves through existing global security thinking. This development not only challenges the supremacy of the nation-state but also significantly raises transformational questions about the central notions of power, sovereignty, deterrence, anarchy, and interdependence. In other words, the topic of this volume's

I

discussion is not a minor side-element of global security affairs, a wrinkle that can be easily ignored or at least isolated, but rather a center-stage phenomenon with major spillover effects deserving sustained and probing analysis. Thus rather than being a small issue largely separated from mainstream discourse on international security dilemmas, this topic provides a novel lens to peer into them from a different angle.

This book provides a comprehensive exploration of the global privatization of security. It analyzes recent trends in privatized security, places the concept in a theoretical and historical context, and explores its causes and potential consequences. Relying on a multifaceted taxonomy of its distinctive forms, brief case-study evidence from eight diverse applications of security privatization illustrates and fleshes out the generalizations presented. Finally, after an assessment of the complexities surrounding responses to security privatization, the book concludes with a brief policy analysis identifying some highly tentative prescriptions about how to manage the privatization of security in today's world.

In addressing these highly interrelated issues, this study intentionally uses the perspectives of multiple levels of analysis. In particular, looking at ongoing patterns from a combination of the international system, nation-state, group (including the view of the private security providers themselves), and individual vantage points is essential to visualizing the full tangle of precipitants, impacts, and solutions surrounding the privatization of security. Too many existing analyses seem to settle comfortably on one viewpoint—most commonly that of the nation-state—and downplay the importance of the others. In contrast, even if public feeling is distorted due to ignorance, the private security provider's belief is distorted due to the filters of self-justification, national governments' convictions are distorted due to bureaucratic inertia, and international organizations' attitudes are distorted due to unbridled idealism, these perspectives merit attention because any management scheme would inherently need to address how each element of the security privatization web sees the costs and benefits of such activity. What appears most central to understanding this complex issue is not just a separate enumeration of the differences in each level's vantage point, but also a detailed examination of the interrelationships among these perspectives, seeing in the process where the points of tension and harmony reside. Because the post–Cold War blooming of privatized security is still relatively recent, misperception is quite common at all levels, including that of state regimes themselves.

Among the many tantalizing facets of the privatization of security, this book dissects the implications of the dilution of the state's monopoly on violence. It turns out that this development is something of a lightning rod for the clash between the realist emphasis on state sovereignty and the liberal internationalist emphasis on globalized cooperation. This issue also serves as a mirror for the widespread fears associated with a growing sense of anarchy on the domestic and international levels, with neither national governments nor international organizations able to address the rampant sense of insecurity directly.

This volume's thrust is distinctive in undertaking a largely conceptual, broadly integrative study of security privatization. Most writings on the subject look at only some of the pieces of the complex puzzle involved, dealing only with, for example, government outsourcing of military functions, mercenaries or private military companies, arms proliferation among the general population, gated communities and private police forces, or militia, vigilante, and gang activities. Many studies focus exclusively on private military activity undertaken by a few companies (particularly Executive Outcomes) in only limited parts of the world (particularly Africa). Many of the prevailing assessments overlook key responses to danger, including, for instance, the provision of privatized security by indigenous sources to cope with domestic threats to citizen safety. While this book's orientation runs the risk of being shallow and overgeneralized in spots, it has the distinct benefits of being able to highlight the parallels among the differing facets of the topic, integrate insights from many different contexts to facilitate new understandings, and most broadly to stimulate fresh thinking on an issue that desperately cries out for sustained and systematic attention from the international community.

Rather than simply summarizing existing perspectives on the privatization of security, the aspiration here is to provide new insight and—most importantly—raise new questions about controversies surrounding this phenomenon. Even though considerable uncertainty surrounds the scope, nature, and implications of security privatization in today's world, showing more clearly where conceptual tensions and contradictions lie and alternative paths for addressing them seems both necessary and possible at this point. Our analytical frameworks for grappling with this issue have simply been inadequate thus far to capture its complexity.

Dispassionate assessment of the privatization of security appears to be particularly urgent because of the prevalence of polemical stereotypes and closed-minded judgments both for and against this trend. Critics see all privatized security personnel as disruptive, involving rabid mercenary "dogs of war" who exploit violence for personal gain, serve as agents for unsavory powers, or thoughtlessly promote repression, turmoil, and human-rights violations. On the other hand, many private security service providers see themselves as just another business fulfilling client needs in a manner requiring no special attention, and many government officials privately voice a strong belief that privatized security provides stability and saves lives in areas where nothing else would do the trick. These ideologically tinged disagreements reflect fundamental differences even on how to define and subdivide the phenomenon of security privatization.

Attempting to present a balanced analysis is a daunting task when dealing with an issue where reliable empirical information is so scarce. Like many other vitally important security issues, it is impossible to get a solid and comprehensive global picture of even the full scope and nature of security privatization, let alone its impact within affected countries and on international relations. This predicament creates a truly monumental temptation to read selectively the anecdotal data that are available in such a way as to reinforce preexisting prejudices and suspicions. Since from the outset it appears clear that the privatization of security is inherently neither a uniform blessing nor a uniform curse, the emphasis throughout this book is to take small tentative steps in the direction of determining when this phenomenon has its most positive and negative impacts. Recognizing fully that future data gathering and policy experience may substantially change the nature of any conclusions reached here, security privatization is simply too pressing an issue to wait for an approximation of perfect information to take a stab at an overarching assessment.

For scholars concerned with global security issues, this approach has the advantage of explicitly linking up with many of the current debates, including those relating security to globalization, anarchy, nongovernmental organizations, democracy, anarchy, and deterrence. In particular, this book's investigation should help considerably with explanatory analysis of current security trends. After the end of the Cold War, security analysts have struggled to come fully to grips with the transformed international system structure, involving different forms of instability, threats, instruments of violence, and crisis management. The privatization of security represents one of these major changes, interactively embedded in several others, and studying it can shed substantial illumination on a broad range of post–Cold War defense issues.

For security policymakers, this book's mode of analysis has the advantage of helping them to place day-to-day decisions about utilizing or responding to security privatization in a broader conceptual context, facilitating the identification of overarching principles—or at least the awareness of conflicting principles—to guide practice. This study also provides considerable detail about the short- and long-run costs and benefits of privatized security—specifically from the perspectives of governments, their citizenry, and the private security providers themselves—to help decisionmakers get a quick conceptual handle on the scope and direction of the latest manifestations of this nonstate behavior so as to integrate it smoothly—knowing when to oppose it and when to support it—into both domestic and foreign settings. As these policymakers struggle in a more tangible way to cope with immediate dangers, what is presented here should directly and indirectly aid in their prediction of the scope of possible imminent pernicious scenarios.

The greatest appeal of this volume, then, is for those seeking an overarching, nonpolemical, and unconventional—indeed somewhat iconoclastic—conceptual study of a key coercive element in modern international relations. If your primary interest is having preexisting beliefs reinforced, or in finding out excruciatingly specific details about particular private military companies or actual uses of private military forces domestically or internationally, then you must look elsewhere. However, if you want a probing conceptual analysis of the many complexities and contradictions surrounding the privatization of security, then what lies ahead should keep you enthralled.

1

RECENT TRENDS IN
PRIVATE SECURITY

To set the stage for an analysis of the security privatization dilemma, a review of the recently emerging state of affairs seems appropriate. The overall pattern is "the growing privatization of security and violence" in which "we are seeing a growing tendency of individuals, groups, and organizations to rely on private security forces rather than on the state's police and paramilitary formations."[1] There appear to be three trends worthy of particular notice: the spread of military armaments to the population at large, the growth of formally organized private security outfits, and the increasing involvement of these private security providers in global turmoil (including war fighting, peacekeeping, humanitarian assistance, investment protection, and intelligence gathering). These three highly interrelated developments combine to paint quite a different picture of global security challenges than under the more state-centric, government-oriented assessments that still dominate much thinking in this field. This chapter discusses recent developments in these three areas of transformation, in the process providing an inkling of how dramatically local, national, and international security are changing in the emerging twenty-first century.

Spread of Military Armaments
Among Private Citizenry

For the first time since the emergence of the nation-state, more military weapons are in the hands of private citizens than in the hands of national governments. As Jessica Matthews of the Carnegie Endowment for International Peace notes, "the steady concentration of power in the

7

hands of states, which began in 1648 with the Peace of Westphalia, is over, at least for a while," in part due to ability of private military units to wage war.[2] A shocking statistic is that while national armies have shrunk by about 20 percent, private groups providing security have expanded to a degree that they outnumber most national armies.[3] The United States has an expenditure on private security reported in 1999— $50 billion—that is larger than the defense budget of every other NATO nation; has private security and policing companies that outspend public police by 73 percent and that employ more than two-and-a-half times as many personnel; and has almost half of the roughly 5 billion military weapons available anywhere to private citizens.[4] While national governments still maintain the advantage in actual firepower, since they possess the majority of the large weapons systems, they have the minority of the kinds of small arms used in the low-intensity conflicts that have actually broken out since the end of the Cold War.

Much of the problem here is interrelated with the dramatic growth in the clandestine transfer of this light weaponry across national boundaries: the robust international weapons infrastructure stimulated by the 1980s boom has refused to wither in the 1990s, with excess supply of arms and excess capacity in arms production combined with greater visibility of subnational turmoil fostering intensified competition by arms producers to enter foreign markets.[5] This spread of arms within nations has caused many advanced industrial societies to join with Third World states in becoming more concerned about largely internal rather than external security threats.

There is also little doubt that "the supply, proliferation and use of arms are inextricably linked to the activities of private security groups," and that these organizations often broker arms-transfer deals and arrange accompanying transport and financing.[6] Some argue that the spread of privatized security can legitimize the use of coercion and feed "a cycle of violence in many societies that in turn causes even greater demand for guns."[7] This causal relationship is, however, unclear: Is it that these outfits bring weapons with them—and stimulate a desire for weaponry among those around them—when they enter a situation? Or, alternatively, is it that the presence of arms in an area stimulates the kind of violence and disorder that triggers the perceived need for the entrance of private security providers? Or are both to some degree true? To draw definitively one conclusion or the other at this point seems grossly premature given the available evidence. Indeed, given the centrality of subjective fear, this "chicken-and-egg" question would seem quite difficult to unravel empirically.

Growth of Private Security Providers

At the same time this rather uncontrolled proliferation of conventional arms is occurring, there is an explosion in the growth of private military companies, vigilante squads, militias, transnational criminal organizations, self-defense forces, and survivalist enclaves. These groups have differing agendas, but they are united in their belief that they need to provide their own security—and security for those around them—in a highly threatening environment because the government is unable or unwilling to do so. This conviction emerges from a sense of increasingly unpredictable and uncontrollable dangers.

While mercenaries of all sorts have existed since ancient times, hired by individuals, groups, or even ruling regimes who felt themselves unable to gain desired territory or prevail in battle, the private security groups we see proliferating today are much more sophisticated, better organized, and often are officially registered and sanctioned by national governments. They operate in such as way as to minimize differences from other types of companies, wondering at times why they are subject to so much notice and alarm. Some onlookers feel as a result that "the day of Mercenary Incorporated as a legitimate, even respectable, service organisation may be dawning."[8] It is even possible to classify this new breed of private military companies as "good mercenaries" who choose to fight only in wars where legitimate nation-state interests are at stake.[9]

Private security today is different in many specific ways from the ad hoc organizations of the past:

> Many of today's companies exhibit a distinct corporate nature, including an ongoing intelligence capability, and a desire for good public relations. Their established character allows them to handpick each employee on the basis of proven accomplishments. The companies' goal of obtaining contracts encourages them to control their employees' actions. Private firms have a large pool of qualified applicants, due to worldwide political realignments and defense cutbacks since 1989. And, many of these companies often enjoy ties with major multinational, especially mineral, companies which provide increased funding, intelligence, and political contacts.[10]

Their appearance and manner is completely corporate:

> They are businessmen first. They have plush offices replete with works of art. They undertake a variety of specialised services—training,

intelligence gathering, personal and site protection and, when necessary, they will go out and rout your enemy for you. They sign complex
deals—bartering security against mining concessions for example, or
acting as arms purchasing agents. "We are an international business
like any other business," a pin-striped, bespectacled and utterly harm-
less-looking corporate head told us. "We have highly specialised, in-
tensely trained and thoroughly disciplined teams able to deliver a
unique service: security. The demand for all sorts of security is increasing. We go where we are wanted and where the people can pay
our fees."[11]

Seeing themselves as a "tool that is not only trained to kill, fight, and
destroy but a precision instrument that can save lives, protect properties
and investments, and advise clients in how to safely go about their affairs,"[12] nothing could be farther from the self-identification of mercenaries from previous centuries.

Moreover, these modern private security providers pay considerable
attention to positive external image concerns:

Unlike the vagabond mercenaries who tended to be active during the
Cold War, the transnational security corporations of the post-Cold War
era tended to be highly corporatized, run by managers who did not
themselves engage in fighting. Like most other corporations, these private military companies tended to place considerable value on good
press and solid public relations. They were as often as not publicly
listed, although, like many other corporations in the global marketplace, transnational security corporations made ascertaining the actual
owners difficult by creating webs of cross-ownership and holding
companies. They tended to be about as open as most other firms about
their clients and their services—in other words, not very. On the other
hand, many maintained pages on the World Wide Web that provided a
full discussion of the services on offer. Most transnational security
corporations offered a variety of security services ranging from military training to protecting vital installations to actually fighting wars
for their clients. Importantly, most strove to be seen as legitimate actors in world politics. They fervently rejected the idea that they were
"mercenaries," noting that, for example, they did not sell their war-
fighting services to anyone other than sovereign governments or international organizations.[13]

Rather than sharpening their fighting skills to kill an enemy, these private security providers end up sharpening their public relations skills to
appeal to potential clients.

In terms of remuneration to employees, the modern private security
provider can easily stack up with the benefits that national governments
can offer:

The hard guys are currently employing the hard sell. At a recent arms show in Abu Dhabi, an Executive Outcomes booth quietly competed for business with mercenaries from Britain, France, and the U.S. Topflight mercenaries and military consultants, many recruited from elite military units like the U.S. Special Forces, Britain's S.A.S. and Scots Guards and South Africa's 32 Battalion, can command anywhere from about $3,500 a month for enlisted men to $13,000 a month for officers or fighter pilots. That is far more than most of those involved could make wearing a regular-army uniform, and the package is usually topped off with free death-and-disability insurance.[14]

While there obviously is more long-term employment predictability in working for a government rather than a private firm, that may be one of the few enduring economic advantages left. Indeed, partially due to competition from private security providers, in many Western governments "the traditional ethos of the military as 'more than just a job' has been partially replaced by a corporate outlook, forcing the military in countries such as the United States to market the extent to which military service was ideal training for later corporate employment."[15]

Much of the focus in the media and scholarly literature has been on international mercenaries or private military companies intervening in crises foreign to their country of origin. These groups in particular have experienced an explosion of interest, as over the past ten years private companies have assumed a central role in exporting security, strategy, and training for foreign military units. Worldwide revenues for the private security industry were estimated at $55.6 billion in 1990, have an estimated annual growth rate of 8 percent, and are projected to hit $202 billion in 2010.[16] Each company is relatively small (with an average annual turnover of $5 million), highly specialized, undercapitalized, and operating in limited geographical regions; since barriers to entrance are low, the pattern is rapid entry and rapid demise in a highly lucrative market.[17] These firms have undertaken military training missions in at least forty-two countries,[18] and many have helped directly with combat readiness; the British government, for instance, recently unveiled a plan to have its military forces hire private-sector mercenaries for use on the front line of foreign war zones.[19]

In the United States alone, there are at least twenty legitimate private military companies, with the largest grossing $25 million a year in overseas business.[20] Interestingly, the U.S. companies—which frequently employ former four-star generals—may have better reputations for being restrained and coordinating their activity with home-state government defense officials than firms from other countries such as South

Africa and Britain.[21] Such high-ranking private military personnel may be fiercely protective of their vital role in ensuring national security.

For example, twelve retired senior U.S. military officers protested in late June 2001 through a letter to every member of Congress regarding pending legislation to open virtually all government contracts to federal employees, arguing that passage of such a bill "would cause 'irreparable harm' to national security," mandate "unnecessary public-private competitions . . . limiting military access to private sector technologies," and "disrupt crucial partnerships between the military and private sector, putting missions at risk."[22] The impressive list of officers signing that letter were Navy Admiral William Crowe, Admiral David Jeremiah, Admiral Wesley McDonald, Admiral William Owens, and Vice Admiral William Hancock; Army General John Shalikashvili, General Robert RisCassi, and General William Tuttle Jr.; Air Force General Michael Carns and General Thomas Moorman Jr.; and Marine Corps General Richard Hearney and General Carl Mundy Jr. Even more impressive, however, are the affiliations of many of these people with major contractors providing private security services: Owens is co-chief executive officer of Teledesic LLC, a global satellite communications firm; Jeremiah is president of Technology Strategies and Alliances Corporation, an investment firm with holdings in the aerospace and defense industries; Tuttle is president and chief executive officer of the Logistics Management Institute, a Virginia-based consulting firm that has indefinite delivery/indefinite quantity contracts with several security-oriented agencies; and Hearney is president and chief executive officer of the Business Executives for National Security, an umbrella group of business executives that organized the letter.[23]

In addition to internationally active private security companies in many countries, numerous indigenous legitimate security firms and civil defense forces, as well as less legitimate vigilantes and paramilitary and militia groups, attempt to provide security within the borders of their own countries.[24] Rather than waiting (often in vain) for outsiders to notice a power vacuum or nonfunctioning national-governmental security apparatus, these local security groups often take matters into their own hands simply to keep themselves and those immediately around them from becoming victims of uncontrolled violence. It is interesting to note that, just as with foreign private security groups, these homegrown outfits operate with quite varying levels of domestic and international acceptance.

Some of these groups emerge due to a desire to preserve the status quo, such as protective private security services. A few quaintly describe their activity simply as "selling the business of surviving."[25] In some African countries, presidential guards are virtually private militias, enjoying better pay and conditions than the rest of the military establishment.[26] The logic behind the growth of this kind of privatized domestic protection is quite similar to that behind the growth of internationally active security providers.

> When a nation cannot provide, for whatever reason, enough government security to meet the needs of the nation, private contractors will fill the void. Witness the increase in the number of security firms, bodyguard services, etc. in those countries where crime has become rampant. In 1994, South Africa ended its apartheid era. Their police service, whose mission had been to maintain and enforce the separation between the races, was not properly trained or organized to perform law-enforcement functions. Consequently, crime has soared. South Africa now has one of the highest murder rates in the world. The number of private security guards in South Africa has grown accordingly. Today, private security guards outnumber the police. The same phenomena can be witnessed in places such as Russia or Colombia. In many aspects, these private security companies can provide the security and protection that the government cannot.[27]

In such cases, the populace often accepts whatever security provider—public or private—can more effectively secure their safety. Indeed, U.S. security analysts have argued that "the privatization of defense on the international scene is not that different from a similar trend at home," as in the United States "you already see more and more people hiring private security firms to keep the Third World away from suburban America."[28] Many countries have augmented government police forces with private security providers—including "rent-a-cops"—to help to cut costs and maintain flexibility while keeping order, and in others—such as in Latin America and the Balkans—governments have outsourced police functions to sometimes unscrupulous and marauding indigenous paramilitary groups.

Other private armed groups, such as angry insurgent factions, develop due to a desire to overthrow the status quo. On the international level, these may be elements of transnational ideological or religious groups, such as extreme violent factions of Islamic fundamentalists who want to establish a new protective order completely opposed to the Western democratic-capitalist, Judeo-Christian, dominant global value system. On the domestic level, these groups are often identified as being located primarily in inner cities, but in reality they have become ubiquitous, found in rural as well as urban areas and rich as well as poor parts of countries: from extreme anarchist elements believing that government is intrinsically unnecessary and dangerous to fearful citizens' groups located in congested battle zones where effective government-enforced law and order is rare, these people band together to form private security organizations with the hope of achieving significant change while protecting their own interests.

In many parts of the world, antigovernment forces of rebels and warlords often resemble private armies and are quite difficult to distinguish from state-sanctioned troops. Sometimes groups possessing coercive capabilities even flip-flop in terms of who they end up supporting and opposing. These private forces in many cases dwarf not only standing government armies but also public police forces.[29] With societies now full of armed factions supporting a variety of different groups and a wide range of stabilizing and destabilizing causes, outside onlookers have difficulty knowing who to support and who to oppose.

Privatized Security and Global Turmoil

Within the post–Cold War environment, those experiencing a variety of different forms of disruptive turmoil have begun to turn more to private security providers as a crucial component of the solutions to these problems. While the most common application has been to fight and win internal and international wars, there has been a lot of attention recently to the possibilities of using private security forces as peacekeepers. On another front, in addition to the traditional use of private security providers to protect foreign investment by multinational corporations, lately they have begun to be evident in helping with international humanitarian assistance to displaced persons or victims of natural disasters. The prospect of using security privatization for peacekeeping and humanitarian assistance indicates that security privatization has a potential to move beyond its more conventional realist uses to achieve more idealistic ends. Finally, privatized security is playing a more important role than ever before in internal and international intelligence collection, especially during periods of instability. Figure 1.1 summarizes the overall global pattern of the privatization of security during turmoil.

Private Security and Fighting Ongoing Conflicts

A crucial piece of the emerging security tapestry is the growing involvement of the private security groups in local wars around the world. A common assumption is "during the 1990s, war has been privatized,

Figure 1.1   The Privatization of Security During Turmoil

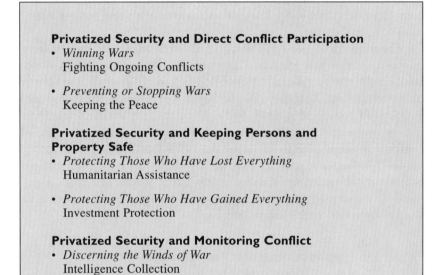

Privatized Security and Direct Conflict Participation
- *Winning Wars*
  Fighting Ongoing Conflicts

- *Preventing or Stopping Wars*
  Keeping the Peace

Privatized Security and Keeping Persons and Property Safe
- *Protecting Those Who Have Lost Everything*
  Humanitarian Assistance

- *Protecting Those Who Have Gained Everything*
  Investment Protection

Privatized Security and Monitoring Conflict
- *Discerning the Winds of War*
  Intelligence Collection

commercialized and outsourced to a degree not seen during the 45 years since the Second World War."[30] With continued reluctance by the international community to intervene in a sustained and effective way in what are perceived as largely internal armed conflicts, military downsizing, and the glut of highly skilled military personnel available, the supply of those eager to fight for profit on foreign soil and the demand for them to do so appear to be escalating in unison.[31] Embattled countries that find themselves low on munitions, training, or able-bodied soldiers can simply go on the international marketplace and buy what they need to keep fighting.

Countries in all parts of the world have recently hired mercenaries, including places as varied as Afghanistan, Angola, Colombia, Congo-Brazzaville, the Democratic Republic of Congo, Ethiopia, the former Yugoslavia, Haiti, Kashmir, Liberia, Papua New Guinea, Rwanda, Senegal, Sierra Leone, Sudan, United Arab Emirates, and Vatican City. There is every indication that the pattern of mercenary involvement in armed conflicts is more widespread during the 1990s than at any time since the 1960s.[32] In the end, without explicit forethought by the international community about the desirability of this trend, private security companies are "assuming an important role in the balance of power both within individual states and in international security as a whole."[33]

Private Security and International Peacekeeping

While using private security forces to fight in violent localized conflicts abroad has been the most widely recognized international application, it is worth noting that perhaps the most ironic use of these so-called dogs of war has been their suggested use in international peacekeeping operations under the auspices of the United Nations. The quest to establish political stability in parts of the world characterized by chaotic violence is quite a long-standing one, and on the surface, at least, privatized security looks like a new potentially effective instrument to accomplish this daunting objective. Futurist Alvin Toffler asked the following question back in 1993: "Why not, when nations have already lost the monopoly of violence, consider creating volunteer mercenary forces organized by private corporations to fight wars [or stop ongoing wars] on a contract-fee basis for the United Nations?"[34] More recently, many analysts have contended that private security can "provide the critical military muscle to make peacekeeping work," as long as they "have a legitimate international mandate (from the UN or a regional organization) and . . . work in conjunction with other interested parties" (including relevant subnational and transnational nongovernmental organizations).[35] During mid-2000, with the United Nations peacekeeping force—composed of inadequately trained and equipped African troops—in Sierra Leone failing in its mission and Western nations unwilling to help out through the commitment of troops, several onlookers advocated the use of private military forces to fill the void.[36]

The United Nations has in particular displayed a long-standing derision of these private forces, treating them as irresponsible mercenaries and proposing an as yet widely unsupported convention banning their recruitment, use, financing, or training. Secretary General Kofi Annan's remarks that "the world may not be ready to privatize peace"[37] and that there is no "distinction between respectable mercenaries and nonrespectable mercenaries"[38] reflects the depth of this opposition. However, even Annan has admitted that, without the use of private forces, the United Nations "still lacks the capacity to implement rapidly and effectively decisions of the Security Council calling for the dispatch of peacekeeping operations in crisis situations."[39] Indeed, for this reason Annan once seriously thought about moving in the direction of privatized security:

> As it happens, the UN did once consider hiring mercenaries. It was in the wake of the Rwanda genocide, when the killers were hiding among refugees in eastern Zaire. Kofi Annan, the UN secretary-general who was then the man in charge of peacekeeping, wanted to disarm the fighters so that humanitarian assistance could flow to the civilians. He appealed to governments for help; they spurned him. So he considered the mercenary option, only to drop it because the UN's member states were horrified by the idea.
>
> The consequence of the no-mercenary policy was that refugee aid went to soldiers, who used it to regroup, provoking the Rwandan invasion that started Zaire's march to mayhem, ultimately costing almost 3 million lives.[40]

It is quite clear that, for some, the possible use of private security forces for peacekeeping has become an ideological issue where issues of practical effectiveness—or more importantly human suffering and death—become somewhat peripheral in any decision about usage.

Affecting ongoing considerations about privatizing peacekeeping are the clear costs and benefits of choosing between using governmental troops or private soldiers under the auspices of the United Nations:[41] the United Nations peacekeeping troops have greater legitimacy, accountability, and public acceptance, while private military forces are less restrained in terms of what they can do to maintain order, have often trained and fought together for years, can deploy where needed much more rapidly in weeks or even days, and usually are less costly. With regard to the Sierra Leone case mentioned earlier in this section, in 1995–1997 the private South African firm Executive Outcomes received $1.2 million a month for managing the turmoil, while a United Nations peacekeeping force composed of government troops arriving afterwards cost $47 million monthly.[42] With the ability to sustain the truly staggering costs of a long-term peacekeeping effort involving government rather than private troops being truly doubtful, a question emerges as to whether the international community is willing to pay this extra cost in money (and possibly lives) to mount peacekeeping efforts in order to obtain the added legitimacy of governmental forces. One central underlying controversy behind cost-benefit calculations is that while "the critics of mercenaries say that paid war makers cannot promote peace in the long run," supporters retort that "this is like pretending that weapons designed for killing cannot be life-saving, even when the weapons are wielded by good guys."[43]

In constraining the scope of future privatized peacekeeping, there is widespread agreement that such forces could address neither the basic sources of conflict nor the most fundamental issues of conflict resolution, as if to assume these possibilities would be equivalent to "using a very feeble lever with which to attempt to move a very large rock:"

> The problem is . . . that they cannot address the basic sources of insecurity, which characteristically lie in bad governance, social inequality, and the highly uneven distribution of political and economic costs and benefits. Their presence is inherently temporary, and they may give their employers a misleading sense of invulnerability that reduces the incentive to seek lasting negotiated solutions to problems of political order. They also have inherently tense relationships, not only with the "rebels" against whom they are fighting, but also with the "national" armies that they displace, and may well be used to control.[44]

In any case, the private security industry simply may not have the numbers of personnel or the capabilities to carry out all by itself the bulk of the global needs for post–Cold War peacekeeping.[45] Knowing these limitations makes any rational decisionmaking about when to use private security providers for international peacekeeping much more difficult because initial estimates of the scope, severity, and duration of a conflict frequently prove to be terribly wrong.

Private Security and International Humanitarian Assistance

A parallel new proposed application of private security forces is in the area of foreign humanitarian assistance.[46] Aid to those suffering the effects of complex humanitarian disasters requires a base level of security for both providers and recipients. While in the past international relief workers were viewed as neutral by conflicting sides, recently they have been more vulnerable, as "violent attacks against humanitarian aid workers have grown at an alarming rate in recent years."[47] Some analysts have specifically suggested that the restraints faced by government military forces in protecting targets of genocide, displaced refugees, or even victims of natural disasters could well receive effective assistance from fast-mobilizing private security companies. Perhaps the trickiest use of private security forces in humanitarian assistance occurs within conflict areas controlled by armed groups and not the recognized government.[48]

However, over past years humanitarian agencies have been concerned about the need to "maintain their impartiality and have generally been reluctant to use them," even though these agencies have grudgingly acknowledged that the presence of private security companies, in some situations, has allowed them to ensure the delivery of assistance.[49] As a result, "to date there have only been a handful of instances of humanitarian agencies using armed escorts, whereas the possibility of private security companies being used to guard convoys, provide intelligence, or protect relief workers has been more common."[50] The underlying widely held assumption here is that "the role of private security companies in the provision of humanitarian assistance should be very limited indeed. . . . such companies may legitimately provide limited guard duties, intelligence, and training; but the fundamental feature of humanitarian operations is precisely their *humanitarian* character, and this can only be undermined, and may well be destroyed, if they are delivered at gunpoint."[51]

Nonetheless, the strains between private security providers and humanitarian aid workers may be lessening. While "sympathy between aid workers and mercenaries should simply not exist, considering the type of people who inhabit both groups and the wildly different jobs they do," a common bond may be developing because "they are both there on the ground, risking their lives to make an difference while the rest of the world simply talks about it."[52] It is certainly too early to say anything definitive about the direction of this relationship, but signs of definite hope for improvement are there.

A crucial question emerging at this point is how, in today's anarchic and violent world, humanitarian services can be delivered abroad to needy yet unstable areas without some form of coercive protection. Is it necessary that those protecting the uprooted, dispossessed, disoriented, and sometimes oppressed people needing assistance in humanitarian emergencies understand the complex and multifaceted deeply rooted political, social, and economic problems that may have contributed to the turmoil? Alternatively, is it sufficient that those doing the protecting simply secure effectively the safety of those under their care until the situation somehow improves? While in an ideal world no coercive elements would be needed in such tragic circumstances, today's harsh realities make the sometimes prickly sensitivities of transnational humanitarian organizations seem a bit misplaced. Although multilateral governmental protection might in some ways appear preferable, that is very difficult to mobilize with sufficient speed.

Private Security and International Investment Protection

Perhaps the most controversial trend in private security providers' role during turmoil revolves around their employment by multinational corporations to protect valuable assets and investments in war-torn areas overseas. While these transnational firms have for decades relied on private bodyguards and security forces to keep property and personnel safe in dangerous regions, particularly when confronting instability and conflict in the Third World, recent expansion in the use of foreign private security companies on a large scale has helped to bring the issue to global prominence. Maintaining the safety of corporate personnel and equipment has always been a high priority; but in today's volatile international climate maintaining security has transformed into a downright "obsession" for much of the world's big business.[53] The tendency of one private firm to hire another for security purposes shows every prospect of growth in the future, as multinational corporations—in exchange for future concessions—finance private military companies in poor client nations where governments cannot afford this cost.[54] The specific pattern consistently is that, "as the big multinationals move into these dangerous markets, they bring mid-size military-security service providers with them."[55]

It seems important to recognize at the outset that many private security providers are themselves multinational corporations, solidly a part of the defense industry. But while most militarily oriented multinationals are commonly manufacturing firms producing military hardware that they then try to vend primarily to national governments, private security companies are service firms providing advice, training, intelligence, and fighting forces to a wider variety of clients. So although recently defense firms have had to diversify away from producing simply defense products and internationalize away from serving simply a home-state market due to sagging demand,[56] major private security providers have experienced a booming business necessitating no such adjustments. In any case, there appears to be a close "symbiotic relationship" between private military companies and some prominent multinational corporations.[57]

The link between private security companies and multinational mining companies, particularly those dealing with diamonds, has become a special source of concern among many analysts. It is not uncommon for private military companies, recognizing that the governments most in desperate need of their services would not be able to pay for these in cash, to ask for payment in the form of mining concessions and oil contracts;[58] the net result is to create a direct link between the private security providers and the extractive multinationals. While a widespread assumption is that such liaisons are dangerous and detrimental to the interests of both governments and private citizens of states involved in such arrangements, such a dire conclusion is not intrinsically obvious.

The interrelationship between these two types of companies in Africa illustrates the complexity of this predicament:

> Multinational corporations already engaged in Africa have been heavily concentrated in extractive operations and include a number of "bottom feeders" that profit from, and correspondingly enhance, conditions of insecurity. The cited 22–23% average annual return on investment for multinational corporations operating in Africa equates with a high level of exploitation. But this in turn derives from a high level of risk, and the inability of much of Africa to meet the governance requirements for investment in manufacturing and services, from which the greatest developmental benefits can be achieved. Africa attracts the wrong kind of corporations, precisely because it lacks security, and this in turn provides the openings for private security operations . . . However, multinational corporations do have genuine security needs, and if Africa is to benefit from its natural resources, these needs have to be met, at least in part, by private organizations.[59]

There is no necessary one-to-one correspondence between the security of a multinational corporation, or any nongovernmental organization for that matter,[60] and the interests of the state.

How this type of privatized protection for private corporate clients contributes to or detracts from state security is a puzzle that remains to be fully explored. When corporations engage in foreign investment and establish subsidiaries abroad, is it really preferable for the subsidiary in the host state to demand special protection from the host state government than it would be for that subsidiary to turn to a private security provider for protection? Particularly in the Third World, where potential host state governments are already having great difficulty executing their primary security responsibilities, it would seem in many ways more prudent for the subsidiary to turn to the private sector to ensure its safety. Any attempt by foreign private groups, such as multinational corporate subsidiaries, to gain special host government protection beyond that afforded to local groups is likely in any case to fall on deaf ears.

Private Security and International Intelligence Collection

Even the use of private security providers in the realm of intelligence within both domestic and international settings is now an emerging reality. The range of activities in this regard is impressive: due to increases in industrial espionage, government and corporate desires to be at the cutting edge of technological developments, and business management requirements for environmental scanning, they are increasingly offering services such as risk-analysis, counterespionage, counterintelligence, information security, and physical security advice.[61] Indeed, the scope of such services offered by private security providers is in some cases wider and more robust than that offered by government intelligence operations in these companies' home states. The use of privatized security in intelligence seems particularly prevalent during periods of national and international instability.

Among the "peace support" operations currently ongoing in Kosovo, foreign private security companies are providing key intelligence. The United Nations Security Council has recently decided to use private intelligence companies to bolster its ability to enforce UN sanctions and reduce its reliance on Western governmental intelligence agencies. More specifically, a Security Council committee monitoring sanctions violations in Angola has hired Kroll Associates, a U.S. corporate security company, for nearly $100,000 to trace the financial assets of UNITA rebel leader Jonas Savimbi; and United Nations weapons inspectors discussed with Space Imaging Inc., a U.S. satellite-imaging company, the possibility of buying photographs of Iraqi industrial and weapons sites at the cost of up to $5,000 apiece.[62] While national governments and international organizations have for years contracted with private firms to collect intelligence, some new worries have emerged in this regard. At the United Nations, for example, this pattern is particularly controversial because there is a fear it will lead to abuse by larger member states: since most of the private companies involved are staffed by former Western intelligence and law enforcement officials, UN diplomats are afraid that these officials will use their assignment to spy on foreign governments and pass the information on to home government intelligence agencies.[63] National government intelligence agencies are also becoming concerned about privatized intelligence; for example, in 1997 "state security chiefs, alarmed at the proliferation of private intelligence and security companies run by former spies and retired policemen, began drafting legislation to curb these spooks-for-hire."[64]

Aside from issues surrounding whether public or private personnel are better at the art of intelligence, important questions emerge about whether one can trust private security providers not to sell secret information to the highest bidder. Should they shoulder the same kinds of responsibilities and restrictions as do government agencies regarding sharing the data they gather with other companies and with national governments (outside of their paying client)? Should issues of intelligence sharing be restricted by the competitive economic pressures of the marketplace (keeping competitors from gaining access to secrets so as to maximize profits) or by the political pressures linked to security (keeping enemies from gaining access to secrets so as to maximize strategic advantage)? Given how porous many governments' own intelligence operations have been in recent years, the record of private security providers could not be much worse.

Conclusion

Although, as with any form of privatization, private security providers respond more to market incentives than to governmental priorities, the move to security privatization does not appear to represent a major step in the direction of the inexorable global dominance of economics over politics on either the domestic or international levels. Several writers have enthusiastically jumped on this simplistic "follow the money" interpretation of international security issues, arguing for example that the privatization of violence has created "a shift out of the age of geopolitics into the age of geoeconomics, in which trade outranks ideology."[65] This sweeping conclusion seems to be overly grandiose and decidedly unwarranted, for it is still primarily governments choosing to utilize private security providers for political ends regardless of the financial motivations of the companies themselves.

Private protection is still not a perfectly competitive industry with military services flowing unfettered from country to country following the open principles of global free-market economics. What we are witnessing instead, both within and across countries, is the resurgence of an age-old pattern of a relatively small number of private security providers filling the ever-widening gaps in the provision of perceived safety by national governments. How far this gap filling can go before these ruling regimes feel uncomfortable about it remains to be seen.

The preceding discussion of local, national, and global trends shows that privatization is leaving no dimension of government security functions untouched. Perhaps the most important new insight is the explicit identification of the major, potentially divisive questions raised by the newer turmoil-managing uses of privatized security, including peacekeeping, humanitarian assistance, investment protection, and intelligence collection. As an initial step in the investigation of these questions, the next chapter fulfills the need to step back and place the privatization of security in a deep theoretical and historical context.

Notes

1. Michael T. Klare, "The Global Trade in Light Weapons and the International System in the Post–Cold War Era," in Jeffrey Boutwell, Michael T. Klare, and Laura W. Reed, eds., *Lethal Commerce* (Cambridge, MA: Committee on International Security Studies of the American Academy of Arts and Sciences, 1995): p. 40.

2. Paul Lewis, "It's Not Just Governments That Make War and Peace Now," *New York Times* (November 28, 1998): pp. B9, B11.

3. John B. Alexander, *Future War* (New York: Thomas Dunne Books, 1999): p. xv.

4. Ibid.; Kevin A. O'Brien, "PMCs, Myths and Mercenaries: The Debate on Private Military Companies," *Royal United Service Institute Journal* (February 2000).

5. Robert Mandel, *Deadly Transfers and the Global Playground* (Westport, CT: Praeger, 1999): pp. 39–46.

6. International Alert, *The Privatization of Security: Framing a Conflict Prevention and Peacebuilding Policy Agenda* (London: International Alert, April 2001): pp. 13, 32.

7. Michael Renner, "Curbing the Proliferation of Small Arms," in Lester R. Brown et al., eds., *State of the World 1998* (New York: W. W. Norton & Company, 1998): p. 134.

8. Francois Misser and Anver Versi, "Soldier of Fortune—The Mercenary as Corporate Executive," *African Business* (December 1997): http://dspace.dial.pipex.com/icpubs/ab/dec97/abcs1201.htm.

9. Tony Lynch and A. J. Walsh, "The Good Mercenary," *Journal of Political Philosophy* 8 (2000): 141.

10. Herbert Howe, "Global Order and Security Privatization," *Strategic Forum* 140 (May 1998).

11. Misser and Versi, "Soldier of Fortune."

12. James R. Davies, *Fortune's Warriors, Private Armies, and the New World Order* (Vancouver, BC: Douglas & McIntire, 2000): chap. 4.

13. Kim Richard Nossal, "Bulls to Bears: The Privatization of War in the 1990s": http://www.onwar.org/warandmoney/pdfs/nossal.pdf.

14. Adam Zagorin, "Soldiers for Sale: The Cold War Is Over, But the Demand for Military Muscle Is Stronger Than Ever Around the World, Hired Guns Are Going Corporate," *Time Magazine* 149 (May 26, 1997).

15. Chris Dietrich, "The Commercialisation of Military Deployment in Africa" (Institute for Security Studies, January–February 2000): http://www.iss.co.za/Pubs/ASR/9.1/Commercialisation.html.

16. Herbert M. Howe, *Ambiguous Order: Military Forces in African States* (Boulder: Lynne Rienner, 2001): p. 188; O'Brien, "PMCs, Myths and Mercenaries."

17. Jakkie Cilliers, "Private Security in War-Torn African States," in Jakkie Cilliers and Peggy Mason, eds., *Peace, Profit or Plunder? The Privatisation of Security in War-Torn African Societies* (Johannesburg, South Africa: Institute for Security Studies, 1999): p. 2.

18. Justin Brown, "The Rise of the Private-Sector Military," *Christian Science Monitor* (July 5, 2000): p. 3.

19. Antony Barnett and Mark Honigsbaum, "Army to Privatise Key Units: Senior Officers Furious at MOD Plan to Put 'Mercenaries' on Front Line," *The Observer* (February 14, 1999).

20. Brown, "The Rise of the Private-Sector Military," p. 3.

21. Ibid.

22. Jason Peckenpaugh, "Retired Officers Say Outsourcing Bill Threatens National Security" (July 10, 2001): http://www.govexec.com/dailyfed/0701/071001p1.htm.

23. Ibid.

24. Comfort Ero, "Vigilantes, Civil Defence Forces and Militia Groups: The Other Side of the Privatisation of Security in Africa," *Conflict Trends Magazine* (June 2000).

25. Issa A. Mansaray, "Mercenaries: Messiahs of Terror," *Expo Times* (Freetown), June 8, 2001.

26. Global Coalition for Africa, "A Consultation on 'The Privatization of Security in Africa'" (Washington, DC: Overseas Development Council, unpublished paper, March 12, 1999).

27. Major Thomas J. Milton, "The New Mercenaries—Corporate Armies for Hire" (Foreign Area Officer Association, December 1997): http://www.faoa.org/journal/newmerc3.html.

28. Elizabeth Rubin, "An Army of One's Own," *Harper's Magazine* 294 (February 1997): 55.

29. Michael Renner, *Small Arms, Big Impact: The Next Challenge of Disarmament* (Washington, DC: Worldwatch Institute Paper 137, October 1997): p. 17.

30. Nossal, "Bulls to Bears."

31. International Alert, "An Assessment of the Mercenary Issue at the Fifty-Fifth Session of the UN Commission on Human Rights" (unpublished paper, May 1999).

32. Ibid.

33. Abdel-Fatau Musah and J. 'Kayode Fayemi, eds., *Mercenaries: An African Security Dilemma* (London: Pluto Press, 2000): p. 1.

34. Alvin Toffler and Heidi Toffler, *War and Anti-War: Survival at the Dawn of the 21st Century* (Boston: Little, Brown, 1993): p. 273.

35. Doug Brooks, private correspondence, June 4, 2001.

36. See, for example, Jonah Schulhofer-Wohl, "Should We Privatize the Peacekeeping?" *Washington Post* (May 12, 2000): p. A4.

37. Christopher Spearin, "A Private Security Panacea? A Response to Mean Times on Securing the Humanitarian Space" (Vancouver, BC: Canadian Centre for Foreign Policy Development Annual Graduate Student Seminar, April 30–May 5, 2000).

38. Doug Brooks, "Dogs of Peace," March 7, 1999: http://www.post-gazette.com/forum/19990307edbrooks5.asp.

39. J. Slabbert, "Privatising Peacekeeping Operations: A Viable Alternative in Africa for Overextended UN Capacity?": http://www.mil.za/CSANDF/CJSupp/TrainingFormationDefenceCollege/Reasearchpapers2000_02/slabbert.htm.

40. Sebastian Mallaby, "Mercenaries Are No Altruists, but They Can Do Good," *Washington Post* (June 4, 2001): p. A19.

41. Marcus Gee, "Send in Mercenaries?" *Toronto Globe and Mail* (May 12, 2000); Schulhofer-Wohl, "Should We Privatize the Peacekeeping?" p. A4.

42. Mallaby, "Mercenaries Are No Altruists," p. A19.

43. Ibid.

44. Slabbert, "Privatising Peacekeeping Operations"; International Alert, *The Privatization of Security*, pp. 7, 8.

45. Spearin, "A Private Security Panacea?"

46. Summary of Proceedings, Defense Intelligence Agency Conference, "The Privatization of Security in Sub-Saharan Africa" (Washington, DC: unpublished document, July 24, 1998): pp. 1–2.

47. International Alert, *The Privatization of Security*, p. 13.

48. Ibid., p. 35.

49. Global Coalition for Africa, "A Consultation on 'The Privatization of Security in Africa.'"

50. Ibid.

51. International Alert, *The Privatization of Security*, p. 8.

52. Davies, *Fortune's Warriors, Private Armies*, chap. 9.

53. Misser and Versi, "Soldier of Fortune."

54. David Isenberg, "Have Lawyer, Accountant, and Guns, Will Fight: The New Post–Cold War Mercenaries," paper presented at the annual national convention of the International Studies Association (Washington, DC: February 19, 1999): p. 9.

55. Davies, *Fortune's Warriors, Private Armies*, chap. 8.

56. Robert Mandel, "The Transformation of the American Defense Industry: Corporate Perceptions and Preferences," *Armed Forces & Society* 20 (winter 1994): 175–198.

57. International Alert, *The Privatization of Security,* p. 9.

58. Abdel-Fatau Musah and J. 'Kayode Fayemi, "Africa in Search of Security: Mercenaries and Conflicts—An Overview," in Musah and Fayemi, *Mercenaries: An African Security Dilemma* (London: Pluto Press, 2000): p. 23.

59. International Alert, *The Privatization of Security,* p. 9.

60. Deborah Avant, "The Market for Force: Exploring the Privatization of Military Services" (New York: Paper presented at the Council on Foreign Relations, Study Group on Arms Trade and Transnationalization of Defense, 1999).

61. Captain C. J. van Bergen Thirion, "The Privatisation of Security: A Blessing or a Menace," 1998: http://www.mil.za/CSANDF/CJSupp/Training Formation/DefenceCollege/Researchpapers1998/privatisation_of_security.htm.

62. Colum Lynch, "Private Firms Aid UN on Sanctions: Wider Intelligence Capacity Sought," *Washington Post* (April 21, 2001): p. A15.

63. Ibid.

64. "Curbing Freelance Spooks," January 17, 1997: http://www.fm.co.za/97/170197/CA.5.html.

65. Rubin, "An Army of One's Own," pp. 54–55.

2

PRIVATE SECURITY AND THE STATE SYSTEM

Embedding the recent growth in security privatization within the wider context of post–Cold War global security issues seems absolutely crucial to understanding the complexity of the web of relationships involved. Among security analysts there is a spirited ongoing debate about whether national governmental sovereignty is declining or even transforming.[1] There are general suspicions common to both camps that privatized security makes alliances, collective security, and burden sharing across governments more difficult, threats to internal security more frequent, and arms control within and across countries more porous. At the same time, however, private security providers could end up building bridges across nations at nongovernmental levels that cement ties and breed cooperation on arms issues in ways that state-sponsored military forces have never accomplished. In this chapter, I first discuss the historical control of instruments of violence, as well as the spread of privatization across government functions; and then analyze the implications of privatized security for globalization and interdependence, anarchy and political risk, nongovernmental organizations and shared governance, democracy and civil society, and deterrence and power.

The Historical Control of Instruments of Violence

The fundamental underlying theoretical question surrounding the privatization of security is who has, and who should have, the legitimate authority to use physical coercion in pursuit of security. The structure of the nation-state, buttressed by the concept of sovereignty, has control by national governments over the use of force at its core—"the ultimate symbol of the sovereignty of a nation is its ability to monopolize the means of violence, i.e., raise, maintain, and use military forces."[2] Perhaps the primary stated justification for this exclusive government coercion has been the protection of human life,[3] even though historically other motivations—such as keeping the regime in power—have often actually taken precedence. In practice over the centuries, there have always been extragovernmental applications of force at home and abroad deemed by the international community as either inevitable or unobjectionable.

The problem in analyzing the source of legitimate authority to utilize coercion derives from the clouding of temporal standards relative to today's global setting. Under prevailing international norms, who can define what sets of regulations or uses of military coercion are proper according to universally accepted historical principles? The predicament becomes even fuzzier when one considers the existence of failed states, whose governments are unable to manage security affairs; rogue states, whose governments employ military measures both internally and externally in arbitrary ways; illegitimate states, whose governments assumed power under irregular conditions; and corrupt states, whose governments are unconcerned about the security of their citizens. What with the rise in power of well-respected transnational and subnational groups offering security services comparable in quality to those provided by governments, there is a growing sentiment in many parts of the world that the distinction between public and private in the security realm is becoming increasingly arbitrary. The global spread of free-market values, promoting competitive privatization as optimal in all spheres of human activity, supports the notion that security privatization is a progressive step forward, moving beyond the confining and outmoded mantle of the nation-state.

From a political-history perspective, there is no reason to believe that having national governments monopolize the instruments of force is best. It is clear that "for at least three thousand years mercenarism has been a feature, often the major feature, of institutions of organized violence."[4] Long before the emergence of the nation-state, international commerce was solely responsible for its own security; for example, the East Indian Company paid for its own army.[5] Looking at the broad sweep of legitimized violence from the origins of the nation-state to the present, Janice Thomson is highly skeptical about the utility of governmental monopolies on the use of force to promote security:

> The contemporary organization of global violence is neither timeless nor natural. It is distinctly modern. In the six centuries leading up to 1900, global violence was democratized, marketized, and internationalized. Nonstate violence dominated the international system. Individuals

and groups used their own means of violence in pursuit of their particular aims, whether honor and glory, wealth, or political power. People bought and sold military manpower like a commodity on the global market. The identity of suppliers or purchasers meant almost nothing.[6]

Privatized security was consistently attractive over the centuries because it often ended up saving the rulers money and because it allowed for the responsibility-avoiding escape route of "plausible deniability" (a concept first mentioned explicitly in the seventeenth century): governments began authorizing privatized security forces as early as the thirteenth century, when privateering emerged for the first time; large private armies were widespread in the fourteenth and fifteenth centuries; and mercenaries were commonplace in the eighteenth century.[7]

The provision of security was without doubt "the crucial historical variable in the rise of the state."[8] Charles Tilly argues that states arose as a "security racket," "trading protection to merchants and others in return for revenues and other services, and in the process for providing a framework for the organization of production, exchange, and accumulation."[9] In this perspective, such a domestic and international racket would last only as long as the particular conditions making it possible and effective lasted. The advantage of viewing state-sponsored security in this way is clear—the automatic assumption of legitimacy and integrity vanishes.

Despite the questionable character of the state monopoly on violence and the long-standing use of mercenaries over the centuries, in the wake of the Reformation, and especially the French Revolution and its Napoleonic aftermath, concerns began to develop about whether being a mercenary was both dishonorable and demeaning.[10] Later in the nineteenth century, mercenaries went out of style, and states decided their armies should be staffed with their own citizenry.[11] It is no coincidence that private soldiers lost their legitimacy in the latest era:

> To be sure, the rise of the national sovereign state in the last 200 years has served to delegitimize mercenaries and their activities. The ideology of nationalism regards putting oneself in harm's way for one's nation as the ultimate sacrifice for the community; concomitantly, however, nationalism makes the idea of fighting someone else's war, particularly for money, both unseemly and grubby. Little wonder that throughout the 20th century the word "mercenary" has carried with it deep disapproval, even disgust.[12]

The employment of mercenaries thus changed from "a natural element of military life to its present status as a 'scourge' and refuge for monsters,"[13] at least in part due to the political implications of nationalism emphasizing that honor and glory derive virtually exclusively from fighting for one's own country out of a sense of patriotism.

During the late 1960s, in particular, a wave of antimercenary sentiment resurfaced. Accusations of residual anticolonialism were a central fulcrum of this international opposition.[14] Many newly independent Third World states felt that state sovereignty embodying complete governmental control of security was essential to their continued existence. Their underlying assumption was that the West had a propensity "to either condone or tacitly support mercenary operations."[15]

The reemergence of private military forces after the end of the Cold War fits nicely into preexisting historical patterns:

> Foreign forces or mercenaries tended to prosper in unstable conditions, or following a change in the existing order. Increases in private military forces also often coincided with the end of a period of conflict which saw standing armies reduced. Both conditions prevail after the end of the Cold War, as they did in mid-fourteenth-century Europe, when mercenary activity expanded rapidly at the end of the first phase of The Hundred Years' War.[16]

Thus the private challenge to state armed forces in this latest era should not be viewed as surprising or unexpected. However, there is general agreement that "the process by which the state will lose its monopoly over armed violence in favor of a different kind of organization will be gradual, uneven, and spasmodic."[17]

From an economic-history perspective as well, the state monopoly on instruments of violence does not appear to be a fixed component of maximized expected utility. Jurgen Brauer asserts that economic efficiency should determine the choice of public versus private control:

> As from the late 19th century, efficiency and the public provision of security happened to coincide, historically, with the emerging nation-state. But today, efficiency and the exclusively public provision of security may not coincide anymore. I claim that in our time the increasing privatization of various degrees of security functions also is an efficiency response to a different, evolving constellation of constraints. This might well include private "mercenary" services bought by nation-states.[18]

Thus while government control of the armed forces was an efficiency response to the emerging rise of the nation-state when the state system first evolved, such may not be the case any more either domestically or internationally. Moreover, monopoly of force—even when it is fully legitimized—can lead to corruption, especially if there is no opportunity for recall, replacement, and substitution.[19] The possibility at least exists that competition between public and private security providers can help improve quality.

Looking at the conceptual implications of the growing emphasis on laissez-faire economic ideas also helps to explain this historical pattern. With the primary thrust of finance capital directed at "the continuous search for markets," the widespread view of the state as "overburdened and incompetent in matters of political economy" has caused pressures on governments to "download" functions such as security to internal and external private providers.[20] In other words, the dilution of the state monopoly on violence can be seen at least in part as resulting from private enterprise relieving governments of responsibilities they can no longer handle well in an open economic environment.

In theory, of course, economists have long looked at defense as a public good, with nonexclusivity of benefits to the protected population the key justification. The traditional economic assumption has been that governments are best suited to provide this public good for the whole society, with a single provider able to allocate security resources most efficiently so as to maximize public safety. In reality, however, ever since the beginning of the nation-state system, even with completely public security there have been significant differentials in the levels of protection different segments of a society receive, and in many societies certain groups—such as undesired ethnic, religious, or racial minorities or illegal immigrants—have been deemed to be completely outside the protective umbrella of government security. Thus while conceptually privately provided security should be less of a public good—and display more exclusionary tactics—than publicly provided security, in practice the outcome is not nearly so clear-cut.

It is, then, evident from both political and economic perspectives that there is no inherent justification for a state monopoly on the instruments of violence, and the current crop of private security companies appear to be far more evolutionary than revolutionary:

> Security companies represent a reconstituted form of organized corporate mercenarism that is responding to the need for advanced military expertise in escalating internal conflicts. Security companies also present new means of disguised efforts by their home states to influence conflicts in which the home states are technically neutral. In this sense, the emergence of security companies is not a revolutionary development in military and geopolitical strategy but a permutation of

past forms of mercenarism adapted to the demands of the post–Cold War world.[21]

Seeing these groups as an extension of private military activity from the past, rather than as a sharp deviation, helps considerably in developing a deeper conceptual understanding of their security implications. The reality is that "as long as humanity has waged war, there have been mercenaries; only in the twentieth century has the mercenary been vilified and outlawed."[22]

Indeed, when looking into the future, some are predicting a return of past patterns both domestically and internationally regarding the private provision of security. Martin Van Creveld contends that future initiators of violent conflict will resemble those from the pre–nation-state period, including the more legitimate tribal societies, city-states, religious associations, and commercial organizations; the less legitimate terrorists, guerrillas, bandits, and robbers; and the quasi-legitimate private mercenary bands.[23] It is even possible that traditional government armies will disappear altogether:

> The spread of sporadic small-scale war will cause regular armed forces themselves to change form, shrink in size, and wither away. As they do, much of the day-to-day burden of defending society against the threat of low-intensity conflict will be transferred to the booming security business; and indeed the time may come when the organizations that comprise that business will, like the *condottieri* of old, take over the state.[24]

Although this kind of dire prediction may seem both extreme and distant, it accurately reflects some fears of future security transformation by both governments and their citizenries.

Even when sticking to present realities, it is interesting to note that currently there are few if any fully state-owned military security structures, and among European states only Switzerland apparently never employed foreigners as fighting forces.[25] Moreover, it is clear that the idiosyncratic (and often self-centered) individual quest for security cannot be fully satisfied by the state. Many security analysts have thus begun to accept the inevitability of the entrance of at least the most respectable private military companies into the mix of ingredients providing national and international security; indeed, the legitimacy of these firms has been growing slowly over time.[26] But acceptance of this trend and understanding how to integrate effectively public and private security initiatives are two very different things.

The Spread of Privatization
Across Government Functions

The debate about the historical desirability of a state monopoly on violence relates to fundamental differences of opinion about how distinctive security is compared with other policy functions subject to privatization. For some, security has been completely undifferentiated from other areas of governance: all that matters is "that people should be secure, regardless of how security is provided," implying that "private security, like private education or health care, could be made available to anyone who was prepared to pay for it and that the whole sector might in principle be privatized."[27] Others, however, have more conventionally contended that "security was a necessary and inalienable responsibility of the state, which could outsource its functions only under strict supervision."[28]

To understand more fully the context of security privatization, it seems important—in addition to the temporal discussion of its past patterns—to provide a spatial discussion of its current relationship to other policy privatization areas in the post–Cold War era. This is truly the "age of privatization," where "communities are hiring for-profit firms to perform the tasks that have traditionally fallen to government—educating children, running prisons, and even building and maintaining highways."[29] Especially since 1990, Western governments "have increasingly permitted or even encouraged such private actors as relief agencies, businesses, and retired statesmen to assume responsibilities that states had once monopolized."[30]

It is widely agreed that "if any economic policy could lay claim to popularity, at least among the world's political elites, it would certainly be privatization."[31] Generally, the goal of the spread of privatization is maximizing value through competition efficiency, output quality, and effectiveness in services, accentuated by the declining quality, accountability, and funding of public services provided in many areas. One analyst succinctly summarizes the potential benefits as "unencumbered administrative flexibility and concentrated decision-making authority that allows for the fastest technical adaptation and greatest devotion to cost control."[32] Aside from the direct provision of security to populations in need, privatization has spread in recent years to many other sensitive areas traditionally under governmental control, including the closely linked defense industry (militarily oriented multinational corporations), telecommunications industry (especially telephone companies), and transportation industry (particularly the airlines). There have been calls for the deregulation of defense from all quarters, even from some officials within government military establishments themselves.

As with security privatization, the basic principles of free-market economics have driven these developments:

> In the past 20 years, privatization and outsourcing have been the watchwords in much of the developed world. Inspired by the preaching of neoliberal economists who rail against the "visible hand" of the State, governments in numerous Western jurisdictions have increasingly passed ownership of a range of public enterprises to the private sector in order to allow the "invisible hand" of the market to work its putative magic. The handmaiden of privatization has been outsourcing—contracting private actors to perform numerous other functions that used to be performed by State agencies. The result has been what some critics have called a "hollowing out" of the State—a smaller State apparatus doing less than in the past.[33]

The simple underlying assumption is that each security function ought to be undertaken by those who can do it best.

The U.S. government has been particularly zealous in this regard. Indeed, "after having privatized in whole or in part nearly all other government functions, the U.S. government is now outsourcing the use of force" by contracting out the training of Third World armies.[34] The presidential administration of George W. Bush has recently required federal government agencies to directly outsource or perform public-private competitions on 5 percent, or 42,500, of all commercial positions in government by October 2002.[35]

While the results of privatization across these various sectors have been decidedly mixed,[36] the attraction to it as a panacea has not seemed to diminish in the slightest. The positive inertia from government privatization of other functions has helped especially to legitimize privatized domestic security substitution, at least in part because to many citizen onlookers it seems that if it works in one sector, it should work in another; but many advocates appear to forget or ignore that distinctive security focus on direct physical dangers. For example, if privatized communication or education systems perform inadequately, there certainly may be some significant negative consequences; but if privatized security systems are not up to snuff, large numbers of people die.

Linking Privatized Security
to Globalization and Interdependence

The march toward privatized security has a peculiar relationship to the inexorable trend of globalization. It is evident that "the one thing that has characterised the expansion of global markets in unstable regions is the increasing use and sophistication of private protection to assure the control of assets."[37] In the eyes of some analysts, "global socio-economic trends are working to erode national autonomy, if not nationalist feeling," so "in a world where the authority of the nation state is fading before the challenge of transnational corporations, communications, and politics, the era of the trans-national military may be dawning."[38] While globalization occurs mostly in the economic sphere and security privatization mostly in the political-military sphere, both fundamentally alter the concept of state sovereignty.

On the one hand, security privatization and economic globalization appear to go hand in hand for three reasons—maximized international efficiency, reduced state control, and increased proclivity to confront risks. Proponents of both privatization and globalization believe that comparative advantage and competition maximize the possibility that the best products and services—in the case of security privatization, the weapons, combat vehicles, and fighting forces—will rise to the top. The expansion of private security providers derives in part "from broad and familiar processes of globalization and commodification, which resulted in the penetration of the state."[39] Globalization may undermine state governments' own ability to provide security (thus opening the door to privatized security): for example, some believe that the policies that international financial institutions have encouraged developing countries to undertake have the potential to reduce these countries' political stability and public security.[40] Finally, "the competitive nature of the global market is forcing multinational corporations . . . to work in increasingly dangerous environments such as Angola and Chechnya, often at the risk of staff safety,"[41] thus necessitating the use of private security forces.

Growing interdependence, associated with the globalization trends, may also reinforce compatibility here. Because most private security providers operate across national boundaries, and choose personnel based on qualifications rather than on nationality, they are likely to benefit from closer cross-national ties while at the same time amplifying these ties. It seems clear, however, that the kind of interdependence promoted by security privatization is more likely to be skewed than reciprocal.

On the other hand, privatization can be inconsistent with globalization in localizing and isolating what is provided. In the case of security services, privatization can lead to pockets of highly different—and potentially mutually inconsistent—types and levels of security across communities and countries, with numerous gaps in between protected regions and populations. When the impacts of interdependence—such as increased migration—are not well anticipated, people may well react against it by building privately protected social or political enclaves. Security privatization may also lead to inefficient redundancy, in which adjacent areas duplicate each other's security apparatus in a manner that provides less protection to each at double the cost of a unified multiple-zone security system. In this sense, gated communities, county sheriffs, and even nation-states themselves may be highly inefficient in providing the optimum scope for security protection.

Linking Privatized Security to Anarchy and Political Risk

After the end of the Cold War, with the bipolar system's stability based on rivalry between the superpowers disappearing, no substitute system of global order has emerged to take up the slack. Within this context of global anarchy, there is great freedom for forces out for their own gain—whether they be individuals, groups, or states—to violate what is left of restraining international norms and attempt to use coercion to grab what they can for themselves. With no system of effective restraint on the horizon—despite frequent emissions of idealistic rhetoric in this direction from the great powers and international organizations such as the United Nations—these unsavory plunderers of the global commons appear to have nothing to fear as they skillfully move around the globe avoiding apprehension by national governments.

On the surface, the spread of this anarchic activity seems to be only enhanced by the growth and spread of private security providers. Many of these unruly groups are involved in security-eroding "deadly transfers" within what seems at times like a "global playground"[42] across national boundaries, where traditional international rules of the game are breaking down, and they find the privatization of security to be a real advantage. The spread of transnational criminal organizations, themselves using private enforcement systems motivated by profit rather than political gain, is completely in tune with the proliferation of privatized defensive measures taken against them. Gunrunners involved in clandestine arms transfers find privatized security forces a ready market for their wares. Drug runners regularly hire private security outfits to help them avoid capture by government forces. Because of the apolitical stance of privatized security forces, rogue states, terrorist groups, drug lords, and other unruly actors find means of coercion more readily available for their use than they would otherwise.

From another vantage point, however, the availability of privatized security may in the end prove to be the only effective defense against this rampant and uncontrolled spread of anarchic behavior. Many individuals and groups, sensing the dangers of this chaotic environment for their own survival and recognizing the inability of states or international organizations to manage it, have retreated into a protective "fortress" mentality: they have responded by finding private means of security, creating pockets of security within settings that would otherwise be entirely violent. Although in many ways this leaves many unprotected areas where anarchy still prevails, it nonetheless preserves the ability of the people within the protected areas to feel secure and operate within an atmosphere of defined order. In any case, with unruly groups free to employ private security forces to serve their nefarious ends without any form of effective restraint, fighting fire with fire by having vulnerable groups resort to the same kind of coercion to achieve protection only seems to make sense, at least to the potential victims.

Faced with the specter of uncontrolled anarchy, political authority structures and economic profit-maximizing institutions alike confront an ever-expanding cornucopia of danger. To address these threats, both governments and multinational corporations engage various forms of political risk management.[43] In this domain as well, the privatization of security possesses dual potentialities.

On the negative side, the use of private military companies by multinational corporations or governments as a means of managing political risks so as to create a stable investment climate can easily backfire, causing destabilizing turmoil to ensue that is difficult to control. This dismal impact may be particularly likely when the use of private security providers is deemed illegitimate in the setting in which it occurs, and instead of reducing risk its use creates provocative sparks fanning the flames of emotion on all sides of a preexisting dispute. Indigenous populations in affected regions may be especially irritated.

On the positive side, the use of private military companies moves those engaging in it from simply assessing anarchic security risks to attempting to control them. Rather than being vulnerable bystanders—as many multinational corporations have been in the past when confronting political turmoil in host states—private security providers give those who use them a potent tool to avoid the image or reality of disinterested passivity. A critical component of political risk management has always been intelligence, and the international growth in privatized security has caused government and corporate intelligence efforts to move beyond their customary focus on foreign-government military activities to incorporate the far more difficult tracking of private armies across national borders.

In the end, it is ironic to note that security privatization may serve to increase and decrease international anarchy at the same time, depending on whether you are looking at a group inside or outside of private protected zones. The classic security dilemma has one state's increased security lead inexorably to an increase in its neighboring states' insecurity; with privatized security operating under an anarchic structure, one area's acquisition of privatized protection similarly seems almost automatically to lead to the increased vulnerability of those outside of the privatized security umbrella. It is uncertain whether it is preferable from any defense perspective to have security increasing within privately protected pockets of safety while security simultaneously decreases outside of these pockets. From a global standpoint, international protection of citizenry would certainly not be very uniform under a largely unregulated heavily privatized system, but it is not at all clear that the situation would be any worse than in a system where citizen safety was exclusively in the hands of national governments possessing very different levels of both capacity and will to address this issue.

Linking Privatized Security
to Nonstate Groups and Shared Governance

In a manner parallel to the controversy over the relationship of privatization to globalization and anarchy, there is reason to question the relationship between the spread of security privatization and the explosion in influence of nongovernmental organizations in international relations. Subnational and transnational groups of all kinds have emerged in the last few decades, with an impact on world affairs so significant that it is common to describe their authority relative to that of the nation-state as shared governance. Some of these groups are out for profit, such as multinational corporations, and some pursue presumably nobler ends, such as transnational health organizations. Some are open to all comers, such as transnational humanitarian organizations, and others are relatively closed to outsiders, such as subnational ethnic enclaves. Some possess as much legitimacy as nation-states, such as subnational and transnational religious organizations; some possess no legitimacy at all, such as transnational criminal organizations and political terrorists; and some are mixed in legitimacy, such as transnational and subnational environmental organizations containing extremist violent splinter groups known as "eco-terrorists."

From one perspective, it would appear as if the spread of privatized security and of these nonstate groups would go hand in hand. As the central ability to make decisions becomes more shared between governmental and nongovernmental influences, it would seem to make sense that the responsibility for providing protection becomes shared as well on both the domestic and international levels. Many ethnic and religious groups would feel more comfortable providing their own security in any case. Because the nonstate groups have emerged out of a sense of latent dissatisfaction with services the state provides—just like private security providers—these groups inherently do not have much loyalty or deference to national governments, pursuing ends that are either narrower (in the case of subnational groups) or broader (in the case of transnational groups) than those of the nation-state.

Private security providers appear to be uniquely suited in terms of their flexibility of scope and duration to participate in the shared endeavor of protecting transnational and subnational organizations. It is quite common for some nonstate groups to prey on other nonstate groups, and then for the victims—who often experience shock at their vulnerability—to express anger and resentment at national and international governmental law enforcement institutions for not preventing the abuses and immediately tracking down the perpetrators:[44] for example multinational corporations victimized by transnational criminal organizations often have this reaction, and it pushes them even more quickly toward privatized security. On the domestic level, subnational groups often feel that they receive inadequate attention or resources from the national government, and as a result private security providers might seem to be a sound fit here as well to fill a perceived protection gap.

From another perspective, however, a very different set of conclusions emerges. Because the proliferation of nonstate groups is seen as threatening by many national governments, some of these regimes have used private security providers as a means of limiting or squashing altogether the disruptive influence of these internal and external nongovernmental forces. The use of private military forces to suppress internal revolts by angry subnational groups in the Third World is a case in point. So while security privatization might be compatible with the diffusion of nonstate influence for those subnational and transnational groups seeking to preserve the status quo, huge incompatibilities might emerge when dealing with those groups seeking to overturn—especially through violent means—the established global order. Even when non-state groups and private security providers are not at odds, different understandings of what shared governance means in actual operation can create friction. Moreover, from a broad systemic perspective this authority sharing could easily create a dire scenario for global stability, where the world becomes full of so many different groups with significant coercive potential (fueled by support from private security companies) that maintaining peace or even a cease-fire in the long run becomes exceedingly difficult.

At the very least, significant questions emerge—from the vantage point of smooth international system functioning—about the implications when nongovernmental organizations hire private security providers:

> What is the relationship between state interests and nongovernmental organization interests? Are issue oriented nongovernmental organizations that face security problems in a good position to insure that a military firm will give them appropriate services? Who is the nongovernmental organization ultimately accountable to? Is it their supporters, their donors, the country in which they are citizens, the country in which they operate, or is it some combination?[45]

The answers to these thorny questions, which reflect the huge security uncertainties surrounding the role of nongovernmental organizations in international relations, have the potential to pose significant disruption in a state-centric system. Nonstate groups' incentives and capabilities regarding effective monitoring of private security providers they hire in many senses seem minimal.

Linking Privatized Security to Democracy and Civil Society

Perhaps more than any other global trend, there is reason to question the relationship between the growth in privatized security in the 1990s and the global spread of democracy since the end of the Cold War in 1989. The most natural initial conclusion is that the two trends are at odds with one another, with the possession of coercion in substantial quantities—facilitated by the widespread availability of private military forces from either at home or abroad—able to undermine and ultimately thwart the peaceful functioning of democratic decisionmaking.

Indeed, some view the connections tying private military forces to the proliferation of small arms and the growth of mining conglomerates as posing "a mortal danger to democracy" within affected host states receiving their services.[46] Others are concerned that mercenaries possess the potential to actually "subvert democratically elected governments."[47] Still others are fearful that the law and order provided by mercenaries in the more distant past has been decidedly undemocratic, as "many of these people were not only beyond the law, they often instituted their own brutal standards of jurisprudence on the very communities that they were supposed to be protecting."[48] One analyst even reaches this utterly pessimistic conclusion about privatizing security: "Our human rights, the rule of law, democracy—the more these are priced, the less they are valued; the more we allow cost to be the only or primary consideration in assessing the imperatives of public policy, the less will be the protection offered to those who may need it the most but can afford it the least."[49]

More moderate commentators worry that private security providers may have largely unintended negative effects on democracy. For example, such companies may inadvertently permit states to circumvent some vital democratic policymaking processes within these firms' home states:

> In other words, to the degree there seems to be an accountability issue, it appears to arise around the state skirting public debate rather than the firm skirting state control. The availability of these firms and the services they offer may allow governments to avoid traditional processes in the creation of foreign policy. It is simply more cumbersome and opens up more public debate when countries send national troops abroad. Sending a for-profit company is easier.[50]

The unintentional nature of this sidestepping of democratic processes unfortunately does not reduce the potential perniciousness of its impact, even though whether public debate actually improves foreign policy is, of course, open to question.

Democracy has traditionally incorporated a whole series of checks and balances to restrain government military forces, but these seem largely inapplicable to either domestic or foreign private military forces. The purpose of these restraints is to ensure that the military does the will of the people, more specifically that it "does not undermine the political process, usurp the authority of government, abuse the rights of citizens, and exercise excessive force."[51] Delineating these controls (in this case, in postapartheid South Africa, though they are similar in many other advanced democracies, including the United States) demonstrates how difficult they would be to apply to foreign mercenaries:

1. Executive control—The military and the use of military force are subject to strict executive control, flowing from the head of state to cabinet to the minister of defence to the chief of the armed forces.
2. Parliamentary control—The executive itself is accountable and answerable to Parliament, which has powers of investigation, recommendation and oversight over the armed forces.
3. Public control—Parliament in turn is accountable to the electorate. The electorate may vote to replace a government whose defence policy or armed forces lack popular support.
4. Legal control—The functions of the armed forces are determined and regulated by domestic law, chiefly the Constitution, the Defence Act and the Military Disciplinary Code. These instruments describe the circumstances in which force may be used; the manner in which force may be used; and the sanctions which apply if soldiers are guilty of misconduct.
5. International control—Armed forces are bound by international humanitarian law, chiefly the Geneva and Hague conventions and protocols. These treaties aim to curb the excesses of war, and to protect civilians in particular. Signatory states are expected to ensure that military personnel comply with international law, and to prosecute soldiers who violate its rules.
6. Internal control—In a democracy the orientation and values of the armed forces provide a form of internal self-restraint. Soldiers respect the primacy of civilian rule, human rights, the rule of law and the principle of political non-partisanship. These values are inculcated and reinforced through education and training programmes; through the conduct and attitudes of officers; and through disciplinary action against personnel who are guilty of misconduct.[52]

Even though the actual application of these controls to government military units within democracies is decidedly uneven, private military providers appear to elude most of them even more.

The success of any form of democracy (and there are admittedly many types in today's world) depends rather substantially on the presence of some sort of civil society in which people accept decisions made by the majority in open elections, even if such decisions are found to be highly distasteful. But in situations where democracy does not have deep-rooted or long-standing traditions, groups upset by a democratically determined outcome can at least potentially enlist the support of private military forces to change the results through coercive means. When national governments monopolize force within democracies, there is a role for direct or indirect consultation with the public prior to the use of that force; but when that state monopoly on instruments of violence dissipates through security privatization, then the potential for chaos ensues, to the point where coercive roadblocks emerge preventing the formation of civil society.

Even within advanced industrial societies possessing long traditions of civil discourse, the privatization of security can interfere in due process:

> Using private contractors may make implementing the engagement policy easier, but by avoiding public debate, such a practice undermines the democratic process . . . Employing private firms reduces the need to involve both Congress and the U.S. public in foreign policy. Using private contractors may make foreign operations easier in the short run, because politicians do not have to make the case to send "our boys (and girls)" overseas. Public participation—including public consideration of the risks and benefits of U.S. military operations—is fundamental to democracy. Avoiding public disclosure and debate by contracting private companies is likely to have long-term political costs.[53]

Achieving efficiency and ease of implementation is often at cross-purposes with attaining genuine popular support.

This analysis seems, however, a bit too sweeping. Looked at from another perspective, the privatization of security—which is, after all, just an extension of the right to bear arms specified in the U.S. Bill of Rights, can be seen as one of the ultimate means to guarantee the proper functioning of democracy. No national government would be able to unfairly persecute, torture, exploit, or kill an undesirable minority group within its borders if all such groups had access to the use of private military forces for their defense. No group of freedom fighters attempting to restore justice under a corrupt or inequitable governmental regime could be snuffed out while the international community stands idly by—as some perceived happened to the Kurds in Iraq in the late 1970s, the students in China's Tiananmen Square in the late 1980s, and to the protesters in Chechnya in the late 1990s—if such valiant groups could count on unlimited private military support (possibly funded by sympathizers abroad). Furthermore, there is some evidence that privatization of security may enhance citizen awareness of potential abuses,[54] and this would certainly help in the functioning of democracy. Finally, given that democracy is still in a state of transition to its ideal form in most parts of the world that have recently embraced it (not to mention within the United States itself), some form of coercive protection is often necessary to make sure that popular elections and governmental checks and balances work properly, and private security providers could at the very least create the possibility that this transition would be a peaceful one until democratic institutions and processes are fully embraced. In considering ways to safeguard smooth democratic change within violent societies with a weak existing regime, there may not be many alternative options.

Linking Privatized Security to Deterrence and Power

The complex relationship between the privatization of security and deterrence is particularly worthy of discussion. After the end of the Cold War, the stability of the bipolar deterrence relationship disintegrated. In its place, considerable uncertainty has surrounded the question of how coercion can contribute to peace. Examining the relationship of security privatization and deterrence thus serves as a critical way to understand the basis of national and international stability.

Changes in the calculus of power are at the heart of this relationship. Several elements, including the reduced ability to judge the military power of a state by looking just at the capabilities of government coercive forces, the proliferation of powerful nonstate groups, and the intangibility of key elements of power, have made the absolute and relative power of states more difficult to determine. Privatized security has a direct impact on this transforming power calculus.

It is easy to see how one could conclude that security privatization could make predictable deterrence relationships both more rare and more unstable: deterrence rests on an ability to calculate the overall coercive capabilities of an adversary, and that calculation is easiest when dealing exclusively with government military strength. The moment one has to integrate as well private military capabilities—ones either already present within a nation or ones that could potentially enter a nation (whether requested or not) in times of strife—the deterrence calculus can become impossibly subject to both convolution and conjecture. Deterrence both domestically and internationally may become degraded the more possession of overwhelming force becomes both less probable and less permanent through the privatization of security. Moreover, while in deterrence calculations government forces are generally considered inextricably supportive of the state—due to these forces' receipt of both training and long-term remuneration from the government— such is not the case for private security providers, whose loyalties could indeed shift with changing internal and external circumstances. In the absence of clearly calculable deterrence, potentially security-threatening bodies could feel much more emboldened to carry out their aggressive plans without rational reason to fear the certainty of overwhelming retaliation.

For weak states, however, the privatization of security may be the only avenue to survival. Predictable power ratios based exclusively on government-sponsored coercion leave many of these countries in a highly vulnerable and insecure predicament. The ambiguity in calculating power ratios emanating from privatized security actually can work directly in favor of these smaller states achieving some level of authority. Because of their ability to gain access to private military forces, particularly when dealing with internal conflicts, it is impossible to ignore such states in a way that would occur otherwise.

The success of deterrence relies heavily on a clear signaling system about coercive commitments, and security privatization can have an interesting impact here. From the vantage point of a state commissioning privatized security as a means of foreign military assistance, it reaps the advantages of increased flexibility in terms of its defense commitment; but from the vantage point of the recipient state, it suffers the drawback of not having a clear globally recognized signal that another government is firmly in its security camp for the long haul. From the vantage point of a state utilizing private security as a means of domestic security substitution, it reaps the advantages of inexpensive cost-effective policing and increased opportunity to use saved resources in other areas; yet from the vantage point of a recipient community, perceived accountability may be far less secure. In both cases the symbolic payoff may be at least as significant as the more tangible benefits.

It is interesting to step back a bit and remember that possession of coercive force—public or private—has not always been the most essential prerequisite to security. For example, the narrow emphasis on soldiers and weapons as the basis for security was not universal during preindustrial periods, where availability of food and water and coping with harsh physical environments were much more central to survival.[55] So in thinking about private security providers as a potentially useful replacement or augmentation for the governmental provision of security, and in focusing on who has control over instruments of violence within a society, we are still operating within the prevailing conceptual paradigm that military power—rather than other possibilities such as economic strength or natural-resource access—is the key to ensuring physical safety. Within the still transforming post–Cold War environment, the centrality of possession of force to stabilizing deterrence and global security may yet receive significant challenges from other ways to ensure the provision of protection of basic needs.

Moreover, exclusive reliance on the use of any form of coercion, public or private, can represent policy failure and indicate a lack of popular support for a regime or for the civilized norms of society. Somehow this very basic reality has escaped many policymakers and individual citizens as they race to construct protective fortresses to keep their way of life intact. So in some sense the frequency of the local, national, and international need for privatized security is somewhat of a litmus test showing the weakness of authority structures to attain law and order through legitimate means without the application of coercion. The desire for privatized protection is thus the tip of a major iceberg of fear, manifesting a deeply rooted breakdown of global safety systems requiring a lot of new kinds of protection—of which private security providers are most prominent—to step in to fill the gap. There is indeed something very primitive about having to resort to threats of violence to remain safe.

Conclusion

This chapter has attempted to underscore the contention that analyzing the privatization of security within a conceptual vacuum makes no sense. Looking at its historical roots suggests that while the specific forms of private security providers today may differ from those in the past, their functions do not; and that their utility in achieving stated objectives—compared to state-sponsored coercion—is becoming more widely attractive. Assessing privatized security in the context of other forms of emerging privatization, it appears that while there are real differences in the way both the firms provide the services and the clients (governmental and nongovernmental) receive the services, neither these differences nor the checkered success of other forms of privatization has reduced the enthusiasm of those wanting to move in this direction.

Perhaps the most important and novel insight derives from examining the implications for other global security trends—globalization and interdependence, anarchy and political risk, nongovernmental organizations and shared governance, democracy and civil society, and deterrence and power. This discussion makes it clear that private security providers do not serve across the board either to thwart or reinforce ongoing domestic and international patterns, and instead have more subtle

Figure 2.1 Theoretical Implications of Security Privatization

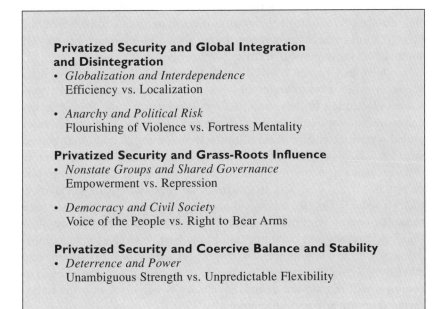

**Privatized Security and Global Integration
and Disintegration**
- *Globalization and Interdependence*
  Efficiency vs. Localization

- *Anarchy and Political Risk*
  Flourishing of Violence vs. Fortress Mentality

Privatized Security and Grass-Roots Influence
- *Nonstate Groups and Shared Governance*
  Empowerment vs. Repression

- *Democracy and Civil Society*
  Voice of the People vs. Right to Bear Arms

Privatized Security and Coercive Balance and Stability
- *Deterrence and Power*
  Unambiguous Strength vs. Unpredictable Flexibility

and complicated interactive effects going in both directions. Privatized security can simultaneously promote global cooperation and harmonization along with global fragmentation and tribalism; magnify the influence of subnational and transnational organizations and the mass public along with suppression of these groups' sentiments; and provide smoother functioning of global and local balances of power along with complete disruption of these balances. Thus whether dealing with the broad coherence of the international system structure, the stability of state-to-state relations, or the ability of nonstate forces to be heard, the privatization of security appears to be a volatile element. Figure 2.1 summarizes these general security implications.

Indeed, as Chapter 7 will discuss, the spread of privatized security serves in many ways to highlight unresolved tensions among underlying values embedded in these international security trends. Precisely because the interactive effects of security privatization on other major global security trends are so multidirectional, internal and international stresses and strains can easily increase as a result of its use. Despite sound reasons to doubt that turning to the use of force, whether public or private, is the best way to confront dangers and ensure survival in today's world, there is no sign that this response is on the wane as a means of coping with these tensions, even if it is clear that the application may have caused them to occur in the first place. As long as global values are highly heterogeneous, respect for authority is highly uneven, and global signaling systems are highly degraded, the threat and use of coercion will remain the central means by which civic order is maintained domestically and internationally.

Notes

1. Robert Mandel, *The Changing Face of National Security: A Conceptual Analysis* (Westport, CT: Greenwood Press, 1994): pp. 1–14.

2. David Isenberg, *Soldiers of Fortune Ltd.: A Profile of Today's Private Sector Corporate Mercenary Firms* (Washington DC: Center for Defense Information Monograph, November 1997): p. 1.

3. Jeff Herbst, "The Regulation of Private Security Forces," in Greg Mills and John Stremlau, eds., *The Privatisation of Security in Africa* (Johannesburg: South African Institute of International Affairs, 1999): p. 109; Robert Mandel, "What Are We Protecting?" *Armed Forces & Society* 22 (spring 1996): 335–355.

4. Tony Lynch and A. J. Walsh, "The Good Mercenary," *Journal of Political Philosophy* 8 (2000): 133.

5. Peter Lock, "Africa, Military Downsizing and the Growth in the Security Industry," in Jakkie Cilliers and Peggy Mason, eds., *Peace, Profit or Plunder?*

The Privatisation of Security in War-Torn African Societies (Johannesburg: Institute for Security Studies, 1999): p. 24.

6. Janice E. Thomson, *Mercenaries, Pirates, and Sovereigns: State-Building and Extraterritorial Violence in Early Modern Europe* (Princeton, NJ: Princeton University Press, 1994): p. 2.

7. Ibid., p. 21.

8. Eboe Hutchful, "Understanding the African Security Crisis," in Abdel-Fatau Musah and J. 'Kayode Fayemi, eds., *Mercenaries: An African Security Dilemma* (London: Pluto Press, 2000): p. 212.

9. Charles Tilly, "War Making and State Making as Organized Crime," in Peter Evans, Dietrich Rueschmeyer, and Theda Skocpol, eds., *Bringing the State Back In* (Cambridge: Cambridge University Press, 1985); Hutchful, "Understanding the African Security Crisis," p. 212.

10. Lynch and Walsh, "The Good Mercenary," p. 133.

11. Deborah Avant, "From Mercenaries to Citizen Armies: Explaining Change in the Practice of War," *International Organization* 54 (winter 2000): 41–72.

12. Kim Richard Nossal, "Bulls to Bears: The Privatization of War in the 1990s": http://www.onwar.org/warandmoney/pdfs/nossal.pdf.

13. Lynch and Walsh, "The Good Mercenary," p. 133.

14. James R. Davies, *Fortune's Warriors, Private Armies, and the New World Order* (Vancouver, BC: Douglas & McIntire, 2000): chap. 3.

15. Ibid.

16. Captain C. J. van Bergen Thirion, "The Privatisation of Security: A Blessing or a Menace," 1998: http://www.mil.za/CSANDF/CJSupp/Training-Formation/DefenceCollege/Researchpapers1998/privatisation_of_security.htm.

17. Martin Van Creveld, *The Transformation of War* (New York: The Free Press, 1991): p. 195.

18. Jurgen Brauer, "An Economic Perspective on Mercenaries, Military Companies, and the Privatization of Force," *Cambridge Review of International Affairs* 13 (autumn–winter 1999): 130–146.

19. Ibid.

20. Abdel-Fatau Musah and J. 'Kayode Fayemi, eds., *Mercenaries: An African Security Dilemma* (London: Pluto Press, 2000): p. 3.

21. Juan Carlos Zarate, "The Emergence of a New Dog of War: Private International Security Companies, International Law, and the New World Disorder," *Stanford Journal of International Law* 34 (winter 1998): 81–82.

22. Ibid.

23. Van Creveld, *The Transformation of War*, pp. 196–197.

24. Ibid., p. 207.

25. Thirion, "The Privatisation of Security."

26. Kevin O'Brien, "Freelance Forces: Exploiters of Old or New-Age Peacebrokers?" *Jane's Intelligence Review* 10 (August 1998): 42.

27. International Alert, *The Privatization of Security: Framing a Conflict Prevention and Peacebuilding Policy Agenda* (London: International Alert, April 2001): p. 8.

28. Ibid.

29. Mark Thompson, "Generals for Hire," *Time* 147 (January 15, 1996): 34.

30. Herbert M. Howe, *Ambiguous Order: Military Forces in African States* (Boulder: Lynne Rienner, 2001): p. 18.

31. Harvey B. Feigenbaum and Jeffrey R. Henig, "Privatization and Political Theory," *Journal of International Affairs* 50 (winter 1997): 338.

32. John D. Donahue, *The Privatization Decision: Public Ends, Private Means* (New York: Basic Books, 1989): p. 216.

33. Nossal, "Bulls to Bears."

34. Daniel Burton-Rose and Wayne Madsen, "Corporate Soldiers: The U.S. Government Privatizes the Use of Force," *Multinational Monitor* 20 (March 1999).

35. Jason Peckenpaugh, "Retired Officers Say Outsourcing Bill Threatens National Security" (July 10, 2001): http://www.govexec.com/dailyfed/0701/071001p1.htm.

36. Feigenbaum and Henig, "Privatization and Political Theory," p. 355; Harvey Feigenbaum, Jeffrey Henig, and Chris Hamnett, *Shrinking the State: The Political Underpinnings of Privatization* (Cambridge: Cambridge University Press, 1999).

37. Mark Duffield, "The New Corporate Armies" (1999): http://cornerhouse.icaap.org/briefings/12.html.

38. Simon Sheppard, "Foot Soldiers of the New World Order: The Rise of the Corporate Military," *New Left Review* (March–April 1998): http://www.igc.org/globalpolicy/security/issues/sheppard.htm.

39. International Alert, *The Privatization of Security*, p. 7.

40. Damian Lilly, *The Privatization of Security and Peacebuilding* (London: International Alert, September 2000): p. 6.

41. International Alert, *The Privatization of Security*, p. 13.

42. Robert Mandel, *Deadly Transfers and the Global Playground* (Westport, CT: Praeger, 1999).

43. Robert Mandel, "Predicting Overseas Political Instability: Perspectives of the Government Intelligence and Multinational Business Communities," *Conflict Quarterly* 8 (spring 1988): 23–46.

44. Mandel, *Deadly Transfers and the Global Playground*, pp. 6–9.

45. Deborah Avant, "The Market for Force: Exploring the Privatization of Military Services" (New York: Paper presented at the Council on Foreign Relations, Study Group on Arms Trade and Transnationalization of Defense, 1999).

46. Musah and Fayemi, "Africa in Search of Security," p. 26.

47. Funmi Olonisakin, "Mercenaries Fill the Vacuum," *World Today* 54 (May 1998): 146.

48. Al J. Venter, "Privatising War" (unpublished paper, May 2000): p. 8.

49. John Harker, "Private Power, Public Insecurity: The Growing Reality of Security-for-Profit," *Ploughshares Monitor* (September 1998): http://www.ploughshares.ca/content/MONITOR/mons98b.html.

50. Avant, "The Market for Force."

51. Laurie Nathan, "'Trust Me I'm a Mercenary': The Lethal Danger of Mercenaries in Africa" (Seminar on the Privatisation of Peacekeeping Institute for Security Studies, February 20, 1997): http://ccrweb.ccr.uct.ac.za/staff_papers/laurie_merc.html.

52. Ibid.

53. Deborah D. Avant, "Privatizing Military Training," *Foreign Policy— In Focus* 5 (June 2000): http://www.foreignpolicy-infocus.org/briefs/vol5/ v5n17mil.html.

54. Pamela H. Bucy, "Privatizing Law Enforcement," *Annals of the American Academy of Political and Social Science* 543 (January 1996): 149.

55. Quincy Wright, *A Study of War* (Chicago: University of Chicago Press, 1964): pp. 20–50.

3

SOURCES OF THE
PRIVATIZATION TREND

As befits the variety of types of privatized security, there are many explanations as to why this phenomenon has mushroomed in recent years. The demand for security privatization encompasses motivations at all levels of analysis, from the international system to the nation-state to the individual. This cornucopia of rationales, many of which are specifically connected to the post–Cold War setting, helps to identify the many different—and often potentially conflicting—gaps private security providers are supposed to fill and the many different tasks they are expected to perform to restore order. On close examination, it becomes clear that the reasons people have for turning to privatized security frequently are connected to unrealistic aspirations and unsolvable problems, where other responses have failed and an almost blind faith develops in this seemingly novel nongovernmental approach. In this chapter, I comprehensively discuss the sources of security privatization, beginning at the broadest global systemic level, moving to the level of the nation-state, proceeding further to the level of private security providers, and finally trickling down to the level of the mass public. I conclude with a frank discussion of the extent to which the current crop of private security providers actually fit the embedded expectations of their clients.

Systemic Causes

The broadest roots of the privatization of security stem from the end of the Cold War. With the breakdown of the bipolar system, states could no longer depend on the superpowers to restrain internal conflicts and provide external security, and many governments found themselves without the means—in terms of funding or skilled manpower—to supply meaningful protection themselves. Because of the absence of a clear and immediate outside threat, defense funding and manpower has declined, with most national governments having significantly downsized their military expenditures, forces, and munitions; even the West has experienced a significant decline in standards for the armed forces.[1] For example, the number of British military advisers declined from 599 in thirty countries in 1987 to 455 ten years later; and the French government reduced the number of its troops stationed in Africa by 40 percent to around 5,000 in the years before the turn of the twenty-first century.[2] In any case, the nature of the unconventional dangers and sources of turmoil that have emerged in the post–Cold War environment have not appeared readily containable through conventional military means.

The cutback on uniformed officers, in particular, left a glut of those possessing military expertise gained in previous eras looking to places other than governments for meaningful work.[3] The release of manpower, weapons, and military expertise from former national governmental armed forces has been particularly evident in the Warsaw Pact states and in postapartheid South Africa.[4] While some have argued that this glut of Cold War military personnel is temporary and will end as soon as the Cold War veterans age, it seems more likely that private military companies will for the foreseeable future "continue to find recruits from national and sometimes international force pools" because "they pay considerably more than a national soldier is paid" and "offer the kind of life that many professional soldiers desire, not the dreariness of routine duties and constant training for an operation that may never come."[5]

Meanwhile the international arena, devoid of superpower domination, began cracking apart at the seams. Subnational and transnational groups began to push more stridently for their own autonomy and for independent influence over the course of world affairs; these groups have been competitors to states as security providers at the same time as they have posed new kinds of security threats not addressable through traditional defenses. A sort of "security vacuum" has become evident, in which the weakening of the state and the withdrawal of foreign military assistance creates a void that private security forces, warlords, or even rogue state armies may fill.[6] In this context, the legitimacy of national governments has been eroding, both because their attempts to use coercion to restore order have not been effective in the long run,[7] and because the justifiability of the times they chose to act in this manner have been seen as arbitrary. Without the clear and present danger of an unambiguous outside threat, many governments cannot defend to their citizens why they need externally oriented security forces. Thus "this new world disorder has given birth to security companies, which act as surrogates for state power."[8]

In sum, a unique confluence of systemic global supply-and-demand trends has made the growth of private security providers virtually inevitable:

> But why did these companies emerge at this time in history? The answer, briefly, is that the conjunction of market forces was just right early on in the decade. On the demand side, there was a marked increase in the number of domestic conflicts around the world: the collapse of both the Soviet Union and Yugoslavia resulted in civil wars; in Africa, the economic stresses of the 1980s manifested themselves in the intensification of civil wars in Sudan, Angola, Sierra Leone, Rwanda and the former Zaire . . . If demand for non-indigenous military expertise increased, so supply conditions favoured the privatization of war-fighting. First, the end of the Cold War and a number of related conflicts had a marked effect on the world's military forces. The end of East-West rivalry led to large-scale downsizing of military establishments all over the world; very quickly, many early-retired officers and soldiers with considerable military expertise and combat training found themselves on the market. Second, the collapse of the Soviet Union had a marked impact on one important aspect of supply: technologically sophisticated military equipment, such as helicopter gunships, that a private actor could never have acquired during the Cold War was now available for hire.[9]

Conditions just could not have been better for the widespread privatization of security.

Nation-State Causes

Demand for private security providers has been emerging from both peaceful and conflict-ridden countries, from both rich nations and poor nations, for a variety of different reasons. It is fascinating to see that, although these companies have a decidedly limited range of services, governments (and other clients) see in these outfits very different means of escape from the limitations they have experienced using strictly the state apparatus. The prevalence of a culture of violence appears to play a role in all types of interest in privatized security, both domestically and internationally. While in some cases this openness of regimes to private security solutions is well thought out in terms of the long-run implications for the relations between the rulers and the ruled, in other instances such is clearly not the case.

Strong Western governments no longer see that it is in their national interest to intervene to achieve stability in distant parts of the world, with an increasingly unclear basis for legitimate coercive action due to the uncertain payoff, the high risks of involvement, and murkiness about which side to assist. Despite the speed with which the United States engaged in the war in Afganistan after the terrorist attack on the World Trade Center and the Pentagon, this quick and decisive intervention is clearly the exception rather than the rule. Many of the opportunities for intervention necessitate a kind of long-term, low-intensity involvement in which even the strongest of these nations' militaries have never been particularly successful in foreign settings. Moreover, the pervasive indifference to these foreign predicaments among these powerful states' mass publics, whose wealth and position make them want protection for themselves (despite their questionable loyalty to the state) but at the same time reluctant to sacrifice their lives for the protection of others in faraway lands, reinforces this noninvolvement.[10]

This great-power paralysis doubtlessly derives in part from a pattern of recent foreign security policy failure. The inability of the United States to achieve a ground-force victory in Vietnam "persuaded a generation or more of American and Western generals that the use of Western and particularly American ground forces in foreign conflicts is a mistake, as body bags arrive back home with all the attendant domestic publicity."[11] This cautious attitude received reinforcement later on, as "for the most part, rich countries [became] sick with the Somalia syndrome: no troops for Africa, not even for Rwanda, not even to prevent genocide."[12] Thus the "mounting human and financial costs" resulting from helping to manage "seemingly intractable civil wars" overseas has created a kind of "intervention fatigue" among Western states.[13]

The leaders of the great powers "have become quite terrified of taking casualties" through interventions overseas, cynically ignoring the plight of others, and as a result private military forces have begun to look awfully attractive:

> An American ambassador in Europe told dinner guests a couple of years ago that his country could no longer emotionally, psychologically or politically accept body bags coming home in double figures. By the start of the Kosovo war, just 15 months ago, that number had been reduced to zero. So we tried to fight a war from 15,000 feet. That taught us the limits of stand-alone air power. We couldn't stop or slow the pogroms, so we creamed the capital city of the guilty nation until

after 74 days a fat Russian stepped in, slapped down his protégé Slobodan Milosevic, and procured a chaotic form of peace. We managed to kill 14 times more Serb civilians than uniformed soldiers and zero secret-police killers. But we avoided casualties and called it a victory. The utter horror of taking casualties has not extended to Britain and France, but is subscribed to by the rest of Europe. As for any kind of involvement in a lethal hellhole in Central or South America, Africa or Asia, simply on humanitarian grounds—forget it. We might use our own troops to extricate our own citizens, or even to protect a massive national economic or strategic facility, but that is about it. We watch the charnel house of Sierra Leone with horror but impunity. Then into the frame, to politically correct cries of "Yuck," steps the professional mercenary.[14]

The idea of victory without casualties is extremely appealing in democracies with a narrow sense of national interest. However, a clear problem this creates is that Third World countries now often assume that Western-government soldiers sent to intervene in conflict situations will flee the moment the real bloodshed begins, further reinforcing in these states' minds the need for private military forces.

Beyond these somewhat abstract concerns about ambiguous rationales for intervention and possible failure and loss of life from such efforts, there are some more practical and tangible incentives for governments such as the United States to stimulate interest in privatization for both domestic security substitution and foreign security assistance. These motivations include both freeing up government military personnel for more important or more sensitive functions that only they can do, and offsetting budget-driven cuts in military (or police) force structure that have already occurred or appear to be looming on the horizon. In the first case, it is interesting to note that prior to the growth of the modern crop of private providers, American government military forces were in many senses overextended, used for purposes and missions for which their training and basic orientation were decidedly not optimal; in contrast, after private military companies made alternatives readily available, it is now possible to fine-tune which security predicaments would entail the use of government troops and which would not. In the second case, both the United States and its NATO allies have in the post–Cold War environment experienced a series of budget cuts, yet in the view of many defense analysts international (and internal) threats have become more diffuse; so in the juggling act to try to maintain the existing scope (or maybe at times even a greater scope) of operations with lower funding, outsourcing to cost-effective private military providers can play a decisive role. In both cases there is an urgent need for a more careful assessment than has typically occurred in the past of the opportunity costs from using government troops and defense budgets directly for managing foreign threats.

Turning from the developed to the developing world, the motivational picture for turning to private protection is radically different. The Third World has long experienced distinctive security problems, involving what some call an "insecurity dilemma" involving major insuperable threats emanating from internal rather than external sources,[15] and this predicament has taxed the coercive management capabilities of even the stronger developing states. Weak Third World governments, often on the verge of becoming "failed states," find themselves lacking the military means to manage their own internal violence[16] and lacking popular support due to conflicting tribes and factions within their own borders. These impoverished countries specifically find themselves unable to recruit and pay for national armies, requiring as a prerequisite a certain level of loyalty to the regime or at least a strong sense of common nationality or ideology, in the face of growing domestic instability and civil wars.[17]

There are now very stiff demands these impoverished countries face in getting outside security assistance, as Western states require certain rigid indicators of movement toward democracy and the World Bank and IMF require implementation of structural adjustment programs that cut into military budgets.[18] As a result, these beleaguered governments may perceive private military sources as the best way to maintain stability because these outside groups are often disinterested in politics and therefore less likely to conspire with internal groups to overthrow the regime. It must be noted that, in the most disadvantaged areas, there is consistently some mismatch in the market between those experiencing the highest levels of insecurity and those actually able to pay for privatized protection.[19]

Given the separation of nation and state within most Third World countries, the level of identification by the domestic citizenry with the state government and the ideology of the regime is often minimal. The demand for privatized security is "fueled by deep-seated problems of governance," as "reflected in the difficulties developing effective and accountable forms of statehood that are universally recognized as the optimum means of assuring public security."[20] Since in many cases the delineation of national boundaries itself was the product of an artificial imposition of colonial preferences rather than of a genuine indigenous upsurge of nationalist sentiment, there is not a long-standing tradition of seeing state government as the protector of society.

In this situation, when warlords or gangs or insurgent groups develop, much of the population is unsure whether these nonstate groups are better or worse than the government itself. Ethnic or tribal ties, rather than public-private distinctions, may ultimately be decisive in determining which side receives support. Within such a chaotic environment, as one would expect, conventional arms transfers are proliferating and seeping into the mass population.[21] As a result, the strength of a national army can disintegrate the moment internal stress appears, and thus domestic anarchy can prevail without the entrance of outside forces, which in today's climate are more likely to be private than public. In the end, "in poor countries the state is all but helpless," and with respect to protecting vital assets "the choice is often mercenary-protected investment or no investment at all."[22]

Thus the combination of inadequacy of internal governmental security resources, unavailability of outside governmental security assistance, absence of popular identification with the state, and prevalence of powerful nongovernmental groups creates a predicament wherein poor countries' governments have few immediate options other than turning to private security providers as the means of ensuring their own stability and, indeed, continuity. The security services these Third World states appear to need most are making "international corporations comfortable in investing in their economies," "training their own police and military forces to provide their own internal security," and "defeating rebel forces that plague the nation and refuse to accept democracy as the only acceptable method for social change."[23] There are simply no short-term fixes to rectify the protection deficiencies faced by most of the Third World; and attempting to turn to long-term remedies for the deep and complex underlying structural sources of these deficiencies has unfortunately proven over and over again to be an exercise in utter futility. In contrast to the advanced industrial societies' less pressing concerns with identification of clear and present danger, minimization of losses, and efficiencies in budget use, for many of the poorer countries of the world the urgency of survival itself is at the root of the move toward privatized security.

Private Security Provider Causes

Perhaps the grossest oversimplification in motivational analysis is the widespread assumption that the rationale of private military companies themselves boils down simply to the pursuit of profit maximization.[24]

Such a premise has led to worries that these firms will constantly switch allegiances and pursue missions viewed as illegitimate by the international community: "given their high-tech expertise and hardware, their sophisticated communication and tactical skills, and their ability to coordinate military operations, these companies could be hired by insurgents or foreign governments to help destabilize a recognized regime or to suppress a legitimate national liberation movement (groups fighting racist or colonial regimes)"; moreover, "in the case of security companies that have links to multinational corporations with significant interests within contracting countries, the concern is that security companies will act solely for the benefit of those corporations by defending only their property, resulting in the creation of semi-sovereign entities to which the contracting government is beholden."[25]

The reality is, however, that many of today's private military providers are seeking global legitimacy and acceptance as much as they are profit. For modern purveyors of privatized security, "what they now want is respectability and large profits," and "they seem to be getting both."[26] They generally contract only with legitimate, recognized regimes, have largely restricted their activities to training national militaries, and have even engaged in low-pay humanitarian work alongside foreign government forces.[27] More than virtually any other nongovernmental transnational organization, they seek the respect that they believe their track record of efficiency and restraint duly warrants.

Even for the most rogue mercenaries who could not care less about global legitimacy, there are motives beyond money. Few mercenaries have achieved riches by fighting in foreign wars, and many mercenary operations have ended in disaster, yet people continue to be interested in this line of work.[28] A recent survey of U.S. mercenaries indicates that "all became mercenaries for similar reasons—the desire for adventure and excitement, the lure of money and the cause was believed worth fighting for . . . the media and political critics stress the monetary motivation of the mercenary, but the interviews showed that money was not the main reason; adventure and the political cause emerged as the primary motivations."[29] Indeed, "one can imagine a mercenary with patriotic feelings for a certain group finding him or herself hired to fight for that group," fitting in a way into a kind of respectable "just war" rationale.[30] Another source reports that "mercenaries in Africa see themselves as messiahs of the people from colonialism, dictators, and rebel factions."[31] Thinking of private military forces as "soldiers of fortune" simply responding to economic incentives and disincentives is thus a gross misconception.

Moreover, there are real questions as to whether there is anything wrong with a pecuniary motivation, or whether the rationale of private military forces is any different from those choosing to go into government military forces. The desire for remuneration is present in virtually all occupations, and it seems rather "empty" to say that even mercenaries with an exclusively pecuniary motivation are distinctive or despicable in this regard.[32] It is quite reasonable to ask whether the motives of even the most crass private "dogs of war" are likely to be "less mercenary than those of current military volunteers (based on the mercenary themes used to recruit them)."[33] While historically in medieval times there were many instances of advancing mercenary troops stopping in their tracks because potential victims paid them more than their previous employers, "there is no guarantee that the motives of professional national soldiers are not purely remunerative."[34] A more modern illustration exists today in a number of Third World countries, where "the armed forces have degenerated either into self-serving corporations geared mainly at enriching their upper ranks or have disintegrated into 'self-taxing' armed units without effective central command whose objective functions bear little relation with security, neither internal nor external."[35] Many question whether "is it immoral to pay someone to fight and maybe die for a cause that is not vital to the national interest"; and some conclude that "if idealism or machismo or money tempts someone into a dangerous life serving his country's values, if not its interests narrowly defined, his is probably a life well spent."[36] Thus, treating the underlying attraction to go into private security work as being totally different from that of established official government forces may be a big mistake.

In the end it is worth noting, however, that it might be better for international community control if private security providers were quite different from government troops and were motivated by money alone. Because the motivations of private security providers may often involve emotional passions surrounding the love of adventure and political beliefs, having these highly freedom-loving groups gain acceptance in the international community or subject themselves to international restraints may prove to be difficult. While not necessarily commanding any respect or even acceptance, coercive forces guided strictly by economic profits are considerably more predictable and pliable than those guided by a mix of multidirectional conviction and undirected courage.

Individual/Mass Public Causes

Perhaps the most deep-seated psychological root of the attraction of privatized security, particularly for domestic security substitution, is the increasing set of fears and apprehensions by the mass public about its own safety. There is little doubt that greater public exposure to incidents of "terrorism, kidnapping, random acts of violence, urban unrest, increasing general crime, corporate crime, and weakened and poorly resourced and trained state law enforcement agencies" has fueled perceptions of insecurity.[37] Whether or not the actual level of violence, crime, or threat has escalated is largely irrelevant, as improvements in domestic and international communication and graphic exposure through the media have caused most people to live their lives in a state of perpetual terror. This abysmal condition—itself a manifestation of the failure of government security provision—is ironically at least as common and intense among people in major powers as it is in the world's poorest countries.

Users of private security services are often motivated to hire them due to somewhat inflated notions—pervading both governmental and nongovernmental clients—of exactly what these outfits can provide for them, as the *London Times* confirms:

> Why are mercenaries in so much demand? Sometimes they simply provide cachet; every Latin American drug baron wants SAS or Green Beret bodyguards. Typically, weak African states, with politicised, poorly trained militaries, are unable either to defeat rebels or bring them to the negotiating table. Mercenaries are thought to offer victory—which is why Sierra Leone's rebels turned to the Ukrainian mafia. Whether effective or not, they are likely to be with us as long as weak states, easy pickings and a glut of potential recruits prevail.[38]

Despite widespread derision of the "dogs of war" on the international level, the persistent domestic media publicity about the foibles of national government and the virtues of "lean and mean" private enterprise has caused many among the mass public to conclude that privatized security will result in "more bang for the buck" than anything the state could provide. Thus the mass public's decision to engage private security providers is clearly not always based on access to complete information about short-range and long-range outcomes.

As people have begun to recognize changes in state protection, many groups have ceased to rely on the government and sought to provide their own private security. Given the declining sense of responsibility to a broader community and the emphasis on immediate self-gratification,[39] particularly evident in advanced industrial societies, a patchwork of tribalism is spreading around the globe: groups focus on managing their own affairs and providing for their own protection and do not care about others (or care about them only enough to keep them out). Public fears about what is seen as the uncontrollable spread of violence, crime, and social decay, the absence of visibly effective state protection, the unwarranted government intrusion in people's daily lives (resented due to the spread of individualistic democratic values), and the rise in power of unruly groups serve to accelerate the attraction of privatized security.

In wealthy countries, people believe the public police are inadequately staffed to provide all of their demanding security needs;[40] and in many Third World countries, the widespread corruption of the police all but eliminates the possibility of official government protection from these dangers. In such settings, filled with paranoia, it is indeed unsurprising that private military companies providing a vast range of private security services have flourished to serve perceived needs both domestically and internationally. With the spread of free-market values, legitimized by the growing universality of economic liberalism, it seems only rational for private groups to fill the pressing security gap left by governments and intergovernmental organizations.[41] As long as people are not particularly concerned about the nature of overall security on the macro level and instead focus exclusively on micro-level protection of oneself and one's immediate group, privatized security has an awful lot of appeal.

Fit of Private Security Providers

All of the motivations outlined fostering a move away from strictly governmental provision of security would mean little in changing the way protection occurs if it were not for the greater capacity of private groups to provide effective security services on the domestic and international levels. Despite their relatively small size, private security providers seem tailor-made for exactly this kind of need. They often possess great flexibility with an ability to create unique solutions for each case, knowledge about the problem area and operational expertise, business integrity, secure confidentiality, and a generally apolitical nature.[42]

Examined in light of more general patterns of multinational corporation expansion, the proliferation of private security providers is quite in tune with international trends. Service industry globally is expanding at a much faster rate than either extractive or manufacturing industry, due to the need for more specialized services that many well-to-do individuals and groups no longer have the time (or inclination) to provide for themselves in a complex global economy; and the provision of protective services—with no focus on the transmission of tangible goods—fits squarely into this privileged mind-set. For a frightened individual, social group, or multinational corporation, hiring a private security provider for protection would appear to be no more remarkable than hiring a gardener to tend to their lawn. Just as with other service providers, security companies do best in this kind of international market when they are versatile enough to tailor what they offer to the extremely diverse set of protection needs from a wide range of clients.

Assuming, as many believe, that winning the type of war prevalent today is "less a matter of applying massive force across a wide front as it is of applying intelligent force at carefully selected points,"[43] traditional government-sponsored standing armies seem far less well suited to this foreign task than are many small private military forces. The "strategic vacuum" left by the West after the end of the Cold War has made the most common type of conflict over the next few decades low-intensity civil conflict, "just the circumstances" where private military companies' "concentrated application of professional violence with conventional weaponry can be most effective."[44] With most private military companies engaged in foreign security assistance emanating from advanced industrial societies, smaller state recipients of their services may believe that such arrangements can be not only more reliable and effective than waiting for other governments to intervene but also reinforce constructive interdependence with the West. Similarly, when considering domestic security substitution, clients of private indigenous security providers often see these protection services as better suited than traditional government police forces to threats from gangs and criminals.

When a government chooses to outsource to private security providers, the attraction today—as with regimes from the past—may result from the state bearing little public accountability for undesired consequences, deaths of citizens, or moral and legal dilemmas about the legitimacy of an intervention.[45] It is widely accepted today that "governments use mercenaries as a risk-free, easily deniable tool of foreign policy: Virginia-based MPRI has extremely close links with Washington—it trains Croatian and Bosnian troops on its behalf—and was in part set up to provide a legitimate outlet for former Special Forces personnel who might otherwise join the retinues of narcotraficantes; Washington has even subcontracted its contribution to the OSCE Kosovo Verification mission to a private company."[46] For the United States in particular, it is possible that "the crucial benefit of privatized military services is lessened scrutiny of its foreign activities, and a level of disassociation from activities it deems unpleasant necessities; with the U.S. populace particularly averse to having nationals fight and die in foreign quagmires, the idea of outsourcing peacekeeping activities is especially attractive to the U.S. military establishment."[47]

In those cases where Western governments do want to intervene internationally, private security outfits give them a low-risk means to do so. For example, missions that the United States would like to undertake for political or security reasons that do not warrant the loss of U.S. lives or that do not enjoy substantial domestic political support (in Congress and the public) could still be undertaken, since U.S. concern for the lives of foreign nationals who voluntarily signed a contract to fight and, if necessary, to die for U.S. interests, and to be paid for doing so, would be substantially less. This utilization of private military forces could also capitalize on the vast numbers of trained, skilled, former military personnel in foreign countries, many of which have depressed economies and have qualified people looking for work.

Beyond their appeal to national governments, these private security providers also serve broad nonstate interests. They provide an easily accessible means for other nonsecurity-oriented multinationals to manage their own threats to investment abroad.[48] For global companies that want for a variety of reasons to maintain a certain distance from their home-state governments, security privatization makes this goal readily possible. For subnational or transnational organizations exposed to considerable vulnerability, privatized security protection involves fewer hassles than attempting to work through governments. Finally, for individuals, the increasing ease by which private security services can be obtained, and the increasing "keep-up-with-the-Joneses" pressure to have such services, makes this move consistently appealing as a substitute for domestic governmental protection.

Conclusion

Thus the supply-and-demand changes surrounding military equipment and personnel following the end of the Cold War, the paralysis of Western nations and the disintegration of Third World nations, the speedy and organized response by emerging private security providers, and the fear-induced hopes by the mass public about privatized security have all combined to foster a groundswell of interest and activity in this area. The impetus from the international system, nation-state, and intergroup and interpersonal levels of analysis have been mutually reinforcing in this regard, a rather unusual finding given the swirl of conflicting pressures within the chaotic post–Cold War security environment. Perhaps most surprising is how tightly intertwined are the privatized roots of foreign security assistance and domestic security substitution. Figure 3.1 summarizes the myriad of sources contributing to the rise of privatized security in the modern world.

Because nobody today has a magic formula for how to establish domestic and international tranquility in the face of sharply differing senses of allegiance and identity, basic values, economic opportunities, political freedoms, religious beliefs, and cultural traditions in various parts of the world, long-smoldering antagonisms are rising to the forefront of domestic and international news on a daily basis. Faced with such danger, neither governments nor individuals would choose just to stand by idly and watch the resulting chaos, but at the same time neither has found conventional crisis management systems adequate as a response. In such a volatile climate, the move toward privatized security seems natural and even inevitable.

It is important to reinforce, however, that supply-and-demand elements spurring the growth of privatized security have not operated completely independently from each other. The ready post–Cold War supply of trained military and paramilitary personnel and equipment has to some degree fueled the proliferation of instruments of force, which in turn has to some degree facilitated the spread of anarchic violence, and this in turn has fostered a growing demand at home and abroad for new ways—such as private security providers—to secure protection. The obvious problem emanating from this tight interconnection between supply and demand is that it becomes more difficult to determine how and where one would intervene to begin to reverse this pernicious but highly interactive cycle of coercion. With the powerful nations of the West capable but disinterested in such intervention, and the weak Third World states interested but lacking the capabilities to undertake such intervention, hope for future transformation in the causes of security privatization appears to be quite remote. As long as people would prefer to find ways to barricade their living quarters to escape from danger, rather than to investigate and address the underlying reasons why such dangers exist, stable and permanent solutions will remain quite distant.

Figure 3.1   Roots of Modern Security Privatization

Systemic Roots of Privatized Security
- *Favorable Post–Cold War Supply-Demand Trends*
  Excess Unused Weapons and Soldiers
  Proliferating Small Wars

Nation-State Roots of Privatized Security
- *Strapped or Incapacitated States*
  Paralyzed Western Governments
  Dysfunctional Third World Governments

Provider Roots of Privatized Security
- *The Lure of Wealth, Respect, and Excitement*
  Pursuit of Profits and Business Legitimacy
  Passion for Adventure and Political Causes

Individual/Mass Public Roots of Privatized Security
- *Societal Paranoia*
  Overblown Fears about Personal Safety
  Overblown Optimism about Virtues of Privatized Security

Notes

1. David Shearer, *Private Armies and Military Intervention* (London: Oxford University Press, International Institute for Strategic Studies Adelphi Paper 316, 1998): pp. 27–29.

2. Captain C. J. van Bergen Thirion, "The Privatisation of Security: A Blessing or a Menace," 1998: http://www.mil.za/CSANDF/CJSupp/Training-Formation/DefenceCollege/Researchpapers1998/privatisation_of_security.htm.

3. Ken Silverstein, "Privatizing War," *The Nation* 265 (July 28–August 4, 1997): 12.

4. International Alert, *The Privatization of Security: Framing a Conflict Prevention and Peacebuilding Policy Agenda* (London: International Alert, April 2001): p. 8.

5. Kevin A. O'Brien, "Private Military Companies and African Security 1990–1998," in Abdel-Fatau Musah and J. 'Kayode Fayemi, eds., *Mercenaries: An African Security Dilemma* (London: Pluto Press, 2000): pp. 70–71.

6. International Alert, *The Privatization of Security,* p. 8.

7. Shearer, *Private Armies and Military Intervention,* pp. 32–34.

8. Juan Carlos Zarate, "The Emergence of a New Dog of War: Private International Security Companies, International Law, and the New World Disorder," *Stanford Journal of International Law* 34 (winter 1998): 81.

9. Kim Richard Nossal, "Bulls to Bears: The Privatization of War in the 1990s": http://www.onwar.org/warandmoney/pdfs/nossal.pdf.

10. Summary of Proceedings, Defense Intelligence Agency Conference, "The Privatization of Security in Sub-Saharan Africa" (Washington, DC: unpublished document, July 24, 1998): pp. 1–2.

11. Abdel-Fatau Musah and J. 'Kayode Fayemi, eds., *Mercenaries: An African Security Dilemma* (London: Pluto Press, 2000): p. 2.

12. Sebastian Mallaby, "Mercenaries Are No Altruists, but They Can Do Good," *Washington Post* (June 4, 2001): p. A19.

13. Musah and Fayemi, *Mercenaries,* pp. 1–2.

14. Frederick Forsyth, "Send in the Mercenaries," *Wall Street Journal* (May 15, 2000).

15. Brian L. Job, ed., *The Insecurity Dilemma: National Security of Third World States* (Boulder: Lynne Rienner, 1992).

16. David Shearer, "Outsourcing War," *Foreign Policy* 112 (fall 1998): 70.

17. Henry Sanchez, "Why Do States Hire Private Military Companies?": http://library-newark.rutgers.edu/global/sanchex.htm.

18. Kirsten Sellars, "Old Dogs of War Learn New Tricks," *New Statesman* 126 (April 25, 1997): 25.

19. Deborah Avant, "The Market for Force: Exploring the Privatization of Military Services," New York: Paper presented at the Council on Foreign Relations, Study Group on Arms Trade and Transnationalization of Defense, 1999.

20. International Alert, *The Privatization of Security,* p. 7.

21. Robert Mandel, "Exploding Myths About Global Arms Transfers," *Journal of Conflict Studies* 28 (fall 1998): 47–65.

22. Mallaby, "Mercenaries Are No Altruists," p. A19.

23. James R. Davies, *Fortune's Warriors, Private Armies, and the New World Order* (Vancouver, BC: Douglas & McIntire, 2000): chap. 9.

24. Musah and Fayemi, "Africa in Search of Security," p. 18.

25. Zarate, "The Emergence of a New Dog of War," p. 78.

26. Francois Misser and Anver Versi, "Soldier of Fortune—The Mercenary as Corporate Executive," *African Business* (December 1997): http://dspace.dial.pipex.com/icpubs/ab/dec97/abcs1201.htm.

27. Zarate, "The Emergence of a New Dog of War," p. 78.

28. Anthony Rogers, *Someone Else's War* (New York: HarperCollins Publishers, 2001).

29. David A. Latzko, "The Market for Mercenaries": http://www.yk.psu.edu/~dxl31/research/presentations/mercenary.html.

30. Tony Lynch and A. J. Walsh, "The Good Mercenary," *Journal of Political Philosophy* 8 (2000): 139.

31. Issa A. Mansaray, "Mercenaries: Messiahs of Terror," *Expo Times* (Freetown) (June 8, 2001).

32. Lynch and Walsh, "The Good Mercenary," p. 135.

33. Michael Kinsley. "Mercenaries: Why Not?" *Washington Post* (May 30, 2000): p. A19.

34. Lynch and Walsh, "The Good Mercenary," p. 136.

35. Peter Lock, "Military Downsizing and Growth in the Security Industry in Sub-Saharan Africa": http://www.idsa-india.org/an-dec8-10.html.

36. Kinsley, "Mercenaries: Why Not?"

37. Alex Vines, "Mercenaries, Human Rights and Legality," in Abdel-Fatau Musah and J. 'Kayode Fayemi, eds., *Mercenaries: An African Security Dilemma* (London: Pluto Press, 2000), p. 169.

38. "A Mercenary Calling," the *London Times* (February 20, 1999).

39. William H. McNeill, "Winds of Change," in Nicholas X. Rizopoulos, ed., *Sea-Changes* (New York: Council on Foreign Relations Press, 1990): p. 176.

40. Edward J. Blakely and Mary Gail Snyder, *Fortress America: Gated Communities in the United States* (Washington, DC: Brookings Institution, 1997): p. 26.

41. Shearer, *Private Armies and Military Intervention*, p. 74.

42. Summary of Proceedings, "The Privatization of Security," pp. 1–2.

43. Al J. Venter, "Privatising War" (unpublished paper, May 2000): p. 7.

44. Linda Lebrun, "Mercenary Connections: DiamondWorks, Executive Outcomes, and the New Corporate Military Market," *Attache* (winter 1998-1999): http://www.trinity.utoronto.ca/attache/issues/0001/back_sec.htm.

45 Shearer, *Private Armies and Military Intervention*, pp. 69–72.

46. "A Mercenary Calling," the *London Times*.

47. Daniel Burton-Rose and Wayne Madsen, "Corporate Soldiers: The U.S. Government Privatizes the Use of Force," *Multinational Monitor* 20 (March 1999).

48. Summary of Proceedings, "The Privatization of Security," pp. 1–2.

4

THE IMPACT AND PROJECTED
CONSEQUENCES OF PRIVATIZATION

Given the recent nature of the post–Cold War move to security privatization and the sketchiness of definitive evidence revealing its full scope and nature, it is extremely difficult to isolate and nail down the exact impact of the local and global activities by private security providers on clients, surrounding populations, nation-states, or the international system as a whole. Even if such empirical data were plentiful, there is an important distinction between the actual consequences of such privatized activity and how the initiators, targets, relevant states, and the international community as a whole perceive them; and for security success these perceptions are vitally important. Judging whether projected results are beneficial or detrimental is also difficult, as often requests for privatized security are accompanied by unwarranted or overly selfish expectations about outcomes. Thus with some trepidation this chapter addresses potential positive and negative effects, with a focus on both the opportunities and dangers involved in the widespread use of private security providers. Crucial areas of impact appear to be changes in individual attitudes, societal norms, state responsibility, conflict-management strategies, and domestic law enforcement and foreign-policy effectiveness.

Impact on Individual Attitudes

Beginning with individual attitudes, two primary areas of concern emerge—the threat to broad community participation and the escalation of mass fears. Both deal with different dimensions of the bond between the individual and the collectivity: the first gauges the strength or weakness of the obligation individuals sense they have to the general well-being of a broader community, while the second covers the strength or weakness of the protection individuals sense they are in reality receiving from this broader community. As is readily apparent, both emphasize subjective feelings rather than tangible outcomes related to both domestic security substitution and foreign security assistance.

Turning first to the threat to a sense of broad community obligation, there is substantial evidence to suggest that the privatization of security weakens individuals' feelings of mutual responsibility because it causes people to focus in a more microcosmic manner on the security of the protected group.[1] In dealing with privatized domestic security substitution, privately protected enclaves seem to concern themselves only with the welfare of those in their group; and in dealing with privatized foreign security assistance, both the providers and the recipients appear to have no incentives to focus on the ripple effects of such efforts on surrounding areas. Often this narrowing of security focus tends to reinforce suspicion about out-groups and a lack of caring about their plight. Ultimately, the result can be a breakdown of respect for governmental authority, leading either to antagonism toward the regime's right to rule or fear of its abuse of power.[2] Equally important, the scope of what people think constitutes their community, neighborhood, or even their nationality may begin to contract, with more demand for tangible demonstration of benefits to merit any sense of responsibility or loyalty in return.

At the same time, the opportunity provided by privatized security causes many protected individuals to feel a kind of comfort, openness, and all-around sense of well-being that they could never receive from overstretched and confined public security services. Though there may be little if any accountability to the broader community or the country as a whole, people who hire private security providers feel that they are getting exactly what they pay for, and sense a tighter link to accountability for effective product than they would with public state-sponsored security services. Whether dealing with privatized domestic security substitution or privatized foreign security assistance, those choosing to utilize privatized security can more definitively shape the scope and nature of the protection they receive, altering it more flexibly over time as their perceived needs change. Indeed, on a microcosmic level such privatized security is much more visible and tangible on a local area than the broader, more amorphous government security.

Perhaps the least-tangible concern about the impact of security privatization is that its presence may engender an atmosphere of mass fear—even panic—among the public at large. It seems quite common to ignore completely these perceptual consequences of the use of private security providers even though there is little doubt that these subjective outcomes are absolutely vital for the presence of a pervasive sense of security in any state. While the preceding chapter demonstrated that fear is certainly a crucial cause of the spread of privatized security activity, there is also the distinct possibility that being more scared may be a consequence as well.

More specifically, the biggest concern about the impact of security privatization is that its spread has a "self-promoting" effect, as its visibility fosters perceived insecurity, regardless of the actual crime rate, thus generating further use of private security systems.[3] On an individual level, seeing a home nearby put up a "Protected by Brinks Home Security System" sign in the front yard can foster a fresh sense of vulnerability among neighbors without one; on a group level, seeing a gated community erected or a private security force employed nearby can similarly make other groups increasingly vigilant to real or imagined threats from outside; and on the national level, seeing a proximate state resort to reliance on foreign private security forces to maintain or restore order can cause regional onlookers to worry more about the contagion of violence from the given state into their own borders. In each of these cases the fear triggered by the visible use of privatized security can easily lead to homes, communities, and even nations transforming into armed camps filled with scared people unwilling to venture out very far from the sphere of their direct privatized protection.

In many ways, this paranoid reaction links up with long-standing theories on "aggressive cues," which argue that the availability of instruments of coercion—weaponry, combat units, and even soldiers—can serve as a trigger to conflict.[4] Security privatization usually ends up making the diffusion of coercive capabilities within the population at large more noticeable than in cases where governments alone possess military force, and from urban riots to ethnic violence, viewing such instruments of violence within the context of a preexisting volatile situation can lead to the spread both of actual conflict and of perceived insecurity. While aggressive cues cannot cause violence to occur without an already existing major instigation or source of frustration, they can clearly serve as the straw that broke the camel's back, whether the private troops come from at home or abroad.

As before, however, it appears that the privatization of security holds the potential to reduce fear as well as to enhance it. For those very poor and unfortunate souls who have never experienced any form of security protection, living on a daily basis with nonexistent, uncaring, or ineffective security personnel, seeing domestic or international private security providers around them can be a ray of hope. Many of these people have long ago given up on their government's ability to provide them with any sort of meaningful protection. To some of them, seeing someone nearby walking around with a rifle is a source of comfort, not an instigation to violence. Similarly, for the very rich, passing through a private security guard upon entering one's estate or knowing one's foreign assets are cared for by extensive security systems usually appears to increase one's sense of security. Thus while fear and panic among the mass population are important possible consequences of security privatization, they are by no means universal outcomes.

Impact on Societal Norms

Turning to societal norms, again two interrelated controversies emerge about the overall impact of the spread of privatized security—(1) the disruption or upholding of social order and (2) the increase or decrease in access to equal protection. In the first case, the protection of a nation's broad traditions or values is at stake, while in the second case the specific rights of any individual or group to equal protection is at stake. Both seem equally involved in whether a society truly feels protected.

The largest gripe revolves around the disruption of the basis of social order. The fear of this interference appears to be greatest when dealing with privatized bottom-up security services provided by gangs, vigilante groups, and private militia. There is the ominous specter of a "might makes right" authority system in which bludgeoning opponents into submission becomes the accepted mode of behavior,[5] threatening the very foundations of democracy (in those cases where anything resembling democracy exists). With private security forces unfettered in many societies by enforceable legislative or political restraints of any kind, the sense of accountability or limits on behavior can vanish. The result can be increased murkiness in distinguishing legitimate from illegitimate behavior and a degradation of national and international norms.[6] Patriotism or a sense of "nationhood" (if present) may vanish in the process.[7]

At the same time, however, privatized security can in some instances be the very best way to preserve the particular traditions and values of a society devoid of other means of protection. Particularly when dealing with privatized top-down security services provided by governments outsourcing security functions to established military companies, non-governmental provision of security may be the only alternative to social chaos. The absence of effective government coercion can easily lead to the kind of rampant violence that can quickly engender a breakdown of the bonds that hold a society together, and without the entrance of private security providers the very identity and existence of such a society can be in jeopardy. In such cases security privatization appears to be one of the only means of giving a society enough breathing room—through the establishment of at least temporary tranquility—to begin to figure out how to restore order later on without reliance on this as yet extranormal mode of coercion.

Turning from the preservation of social order to the impact on unequal access within states, a second debate rages. Critics argue that the more individuals and private groups seek to provide their own protection, the more societal disparities in security may grow within and across countries as security may become more a function of disposable income, leading to a new order based on violence that translates economic inequality into security inequality:

> The changes in the social fabric include major transformations of the social geography with deep social segmentation. Public space turns into commercial centers and private confines, sometimes in the guise of private business districts financed through "private" taxes. Gated communities, spreading rapidly in the United States, in capitals of the developing world, and in transitional countries, are the most visible manifestation of this trend. While the well-to-do social strata opt for self-ghettoization and give notice to the social contract of the constitutional welfare state, criminal energy directs itself against the poorer strata of society living in an apartheid of poverty without the economic resources required to seek protection through the private security industry. The polarization between no-go areas for the public police and the appropriation of public security services by the middle and upper classes is also reinforced by corporate sponsoring of local police forces.[8]

More specifically, in the long term it is possible that "the privatization of security may lead to inequality and injustice because security is available to those in power or those who can pay for it"[9]; and in the end overall societal security may erode as the gap between the security "haves" and "have-nots" widens.[10] While even under public governmental management "'security' has always been dispensed very selectively within both the national and international community, reflecting socioeconomic status, residency, and state of citizenship,"[11] the argument here is that private management may create even worse disparities.

This impact on increasing inequality can be accentuated when private security outfits operate according to a desire to make as much money as possible from political instability. For example, on occasion, "preying on the vulnerability of kleptocratic regimes, corporate armies are repackaging violence in pseudo-market frills, with their eyes firmly

set on creating safe havens around enclaves that are rich in natural resources."[12] The net effect here may be to maximize the rich-poor gap
not only between a corporation and the masses but also between the
corrupt, greedy host-state government and its citizenry.

While it is difficult to contend that widespread privatization of security has a greater potential than government-provided security to
cause visible protection inequalities among various segments of the target population, providing equal *access* to security is a different issue.
First, one could argue that, even when the state provides security, all
people do not receive equal protection: in most countries, the density
of foreign or domestic police or military personnel—and their willingness to intervene in rowdy or violent situations—appears to be considerably lower in economically poor areas, or in areas inhabited by marginal ethnic, religious, or racial groups, than in well-to-do-areas or areas
inhabited by the dominant social group. Second, it seems reasonable to
assert that privatized security makes these existing protection inequalities more blatantly obvious to all citizens than does public state security,
where many still misguidedly believe that all receive equal protection
because it reads so under prevailing law; exposing the nature and magnitude of protection inequalities can be beneficial because it ultimately
can lead to quicker remedial action to reduce the security differences.
Third—and most importantly—following the free market model en-
dorsed by most of the world's governments, the spread of privatized security gives anyone and everyone an equal opportunity to buy protection if they can come up with the money to pay for it.

Posed in this way, access to security is not so different from any
other private good or service in society, as you get what you pay for;
this is arguably more fair than a government security system where people in some disadvantaged areas pay ever-escalating taxes for no tangible increase in protection whatsoever. If some groups exist who cannot
afford this, then the problem may not be inherent deficiencies of privatized protection but rather the unwillingness of lending agencies to provide needed funds to such disadvantaged groups. These arguments seem
particularly applicable to private domestic security substitution where
preexisting inequalities are already apparent.

Impact on State Responsibility

Perhaps the most sweeping potential impact of security privatization is
on the nature of the state itself. There is tremendous concern about the

cumulative impact of the externalization of state functions, of which security is but the latest manifestation:

> While liberalisation and democratisation continue to be sold as the panacea, the state is being virtually hollowed out and little to nothing is left for democratically elected politicians to decide, because the major state functions have long since been externalised. As a result, African states are in a process of steady conversion into Potemkin facades, behind which international agencies and actors are running the economy, mostly in collusion with local elites turned entrepreneurs. This process has been dubbed "the project of external governance." Military functions and security services are only the latest additions to the list of state functions being externalised and often privatised.[13]

Regardless of whether government functions end up being outsourced to internal private providers (as in the case of domestic security substitution), or to external private providers (as in the case of foreign security assistance), the impact on the state government in question is frequently deemed to be negative. In this view, the growth of privatized security and the decline of national governments appear to be inextricably interconnected, with the strength of the private and public sectors in somewhat of a zero-sum relationship.

Some very specific potential dangers to effective delivery of services emerge from the externalization of state security functions to private security contractors. These include possibilities of (1) poor contractor performance; (2) entrance of contractors into specific engagements that they haven't anticipated or trained for and are not well equipped to handle; (3) significant unanticipated degradation of the overall environment in which they operate, becoming more physically dangerous or even subject to attacks from adversarial groups; (4) engagement of contractor personnel in unauthorized or unlawful acts, inviting adverse reactions (or lawsuits) from the public, the media, or the government of the host country; (5) protracted delays or competition-related problems in acquiring the contracts, leading to inefficiencies or gaps in coverage; (6) transformation of the contractors into targets for hostile intelligence services, having agents emplaced who then collect information or even take hostile actions such as sabotage; and (7) unwillingness of contractors to do the work specified by the government for the amount of money it has budgeted or thinks the job is worth. Considered together, all of these ominous consequences can serve as a source of major embarrassment to a national government that has carefully and deliberately chosen to outsource some or all of its security functions, highlighting for all of the international community—as well as unsupportive internal factions—the jeopardy and vulnerability that may emerge from this transfer of protection to the private sector.

The nature of the personnel involved in private security provision may also be a source of danger to the state, as illustrated by this South African example:

> The greatest potential threat to the state from private security companies centres around their personnel composition. As it comprises large numbers of former South African Defence Force (SADF) members and former members of other disbanded forces, they have access to specialised skills and knowledge, and protected or classified information and equipment of the state. In addition there is a continued recruitment of personnel working in these environments. Their activities may threaten the internal security of South Africa should paramilitary or other support to domestic extremist organisations be provided.
>
> The same problem applies to security companies registered in other countries as their main recruiting ground is the same—former military personnel. Therefore, private security companies operating in the international environment are perceived to be directly or indirectly linked to their countries of origin and being used as a conduit for information/intelligence gathering as well as being involved in covert weapon delivery to countries such as the Democratic Republic of the Congo (DRC) and Military Professional Resources Incorporated (MPRI) training to Kabila rebels in Rwanda 1997. Their activities can be seen as instruments of government and may even exacerbate or instigate conflict.[14]

It is hard for national governments to control either the perception or the reality of these possible negative consequences from engaging such paramilitary personnel.

Most generally, externalization of state functions to private security providers may substantially reduce government control because it deeply embeds the financial success of the country involved in the workings of the international political economy. Private military companies respond at least as much to the winds of change in the global marketplace, especially changes in supply and demand, as they do to the whims of the governments of countries in which they operate. National governmental direction of the course of both security and economic affairs would normally suffer as a result.

It is possible, of course, to shrug off this notion of "the hollowing out of the state" as being simply minor changes in government functions that in no way signify the deterioration of state authority. From a long-term historical viewpoint, nation-states have undergone a wide variety of adjustments in the services they perform for their societies:

some are in reaction to changing internal demands, others are in response to external drains on resources, and still others are as a result of the emergence or disappearance of nongovernmental groups offering to provide similar functions. To many, the emergence of private subnational and transnational organizations seeming to usurp the role of the state may instead simply transform both the expectations and the reality of what the state performs for the society, altering in the process the social contract between ruling regimes and their citizenry.

One could also argue the case that the consequences of this "external governance" induced by security privatization are ultimately beneficial. If there are outfits outside of a government that can more efficiently and effectively provide security services, in the minds not only of the clients protected by these services but also of the governments who outsource them, then why should not these functions be privatized? Following a variant of comparative advantage, under such an arrangement the government can provide those security services that it does best while private companies provide those services that they do best, and the net result can be that those protected—the citizenry—can get the best of all possible worlds. An offshoot of the infamous (but grossly oversimplified) "guns-versus-butter" argument could even contend here that such a reallocation of resources would allow governments to redirect some monies spent for defense into beneficial social services. A crucial underlying premise of this argument is that people in all countries are relatively indifferent to the source of their protection—public or private—as long as they receive it in adequate quantities.

Impact on Conflict-Management Strategies

Moving to conflict-management strategies, many worry that security privatization makes violence the tool of choice domestically and internationally. The readily available private armies appear to make the resort to force more attractive for a variety of belligerent groups,[15] and even status quo organizations attempting to maintain order within a society might be more prone to resort to coercive solutions if private military forces are readily available. The sanctioning by Western powers of the use of private coercion to achieve desired ends sets an interesting—and potentially destabilizing—role model for the Third World. The visibility of instruments of violence—including weaponry, combat units, and armed personnel—in many people's minds makes the resort to physical coercion a more natural and immediate option.

A related unintended consequence of security privatization on conflict management may be to militarize the official governmental police or army forces to keep up with prevailing coercion thresholds.[16] One of the ironic problems these dynamics create is that the outcome of uses of force both internally and externally may become more indeterminate: possessing overwhelming force sufficient to attain one's objectives appears to be less likely when a weak opponent can compensate for its inadequacies quickly by hiring a private army, making the predictable workings of stable conflict-preventing deterrence relationships seem less likely. Thus in a worst-case scenario, whether dealing with domestic security substitution or foreign security assistance, the introduction of private forces can lead to an arms-race-like escalation of coercive capabilities by each of the sides to a conflict, with the ability of any of the parties to achieve its objectives at any particular point in time near zero. For those who would argue that responsible private military companies would not choose to enter the fray unless they could see a clear path to victory or identify a side whose goals and tactics were worthy of support, the nature of post–Cold War clashes is such that clear-cut discriminations are almost nonexistent in most of those cases where privatized help would be solicited.

The possibility also exists that legitimizing the use of violence by having a government request internal or external private security assistance, and thus employing those not subject to the strict restraints normally applied to government armies or police forces, can escalate the occurrence of unlawful activity and thus increase turmoil within societies. Several analysts feel that the presence of privatized security increases the frequency and severity of human-rights violations or other crimes against humanity.[17] Others argue that private security providers not only may result from the spread of conventional arms but also may themselves accelerate weapons proliferation, expressing a concern that a dangerous liaison may emerge between private security firms and covert and overt arms suppliers (including governments) searching for markets for arms.[18] Finally, some onlookers link the most dangerous mercenaries to all sorts of illicit criminal activities including drug trafficking, illegal extraction of resources, and even acts of international terrorism[19]; this possibility received some credence when a Mexican drug-trafficking organization recently hired mercenaries to train cartel security forces in advanced military tactics and surveillance techniques.[20]

The underlying pessimistic assumption here is that those who would choose to work for private military providers would either be scoundrels or—at the very least—possess significantly lower standards of performance or desires to adhere to prevailing norms. When such individuals were given government sanctioning to go into an area and stop a conflict, achieve victory for one side, or simply maintain order, this way of thinking would presume that they would likely ignore whatever restrictions or terms of agreement were specified beforehand and simply consider the situation a "no-holds-barred" carte blanche pass to do whatever barbarous acts they deemed necessary to achieve the objectives for which they were being paid. Even worse, this suspicious mind-set assumes that, beyond what is necessary to achieve their military mission, these private groups would inescapably wander into other unrelated areas of unsavory activity once given the mandate to be present and active within a society.

But once again these dire predictions of dastardly consequences emerging from the use of private security providers may be ignoring some key benefits. In many of the countries where privatized foreign security assistance is requested, there is little chance that the entrance of private forces will increase the predisposition to use violence to solve problems because the societies are already completely wracked with uncontrolled aggression; instead, such external forces appear to many to be the only chance for peace and a cessation of violence. For nations pursuing domestic security substitution, there appears to be little evidence that augmenting public police forces through the use of private security providers raises either the actual level of violence or the perceived visibility and acceptability of violence within targeted areas. The challenges of maintaining overwhelming force so as to be able to accomplish objectives would appear to be an equal obstacle in modern conflicts whether or not privatized security were involved, as the flow of high-powered weaponry both within and across countries—with the potential to change balances of coercive capabilities extremely rapidly—is present virtually everywhere in the world.

As to the possibility that the use of private security providers will result in such forces engaging illicit and heinous acts violating national and international norms and laws in the course of their provision of military services, a few compelling responses need voicing. First, the recent record of officially recognized private military companies—as opposed to the record farther back in history of savage bands of mercenaries—has been relatively spotless, whether those contracted are simply providing security advice or actually fighting in armed battles. Second, for both domestic security substitution and foreign security assistance, the record of government-sponsored military and police forces all over the world is far from being universally commendable, with both personal and institutional corruption significantly tainting the record. Third, the comparative preparedness of private and public forces for their coercive tasks seems at least on the surface virtually impossible to evaluate from a systematic global perspective. Finally, regardless of the validity of any of the concerns expressed, in the most severe cases of uncontrollable turmoil, privatized security services may be the only option with any hope of restoring order, filling a void where existing government authorities are fearful of treading due to political, military, or financial costs.[21]

Impact on Domestic Law Enforcement Effectiveness

Choosing specifically to utilize privatized security domestically to augment or even replace police force raises the specter of some special negative consequences. Most importantly, the growth of privatized security has the potential not only to weaken the state but also to serve as an impetus toward "slow-motion demobilization" of its official police and military forces, leading them to try to sell their services to some group or live on extortion themselves:

> In response to the ensuing general insecurity, all social actors take up their own defence against criminality. This privatisation of security polarises the society because security is converted into a commodity. It can be purchased in the regular economy from a private security company, in a gray area by buying off state agents, in the informal sector by militianisation, or in the criminal sector by paying a racketeer. Once violence has begun to regulate economic transactions, security becomes a major occupation because it is a functional precondition for any transaction. A private security escalation is the logical consequence, which eventually takes on the dimension of an internal arms race encompassing mainly small arms. The productivity of the economy, including the criminal and informal sectors, rapidly contracts further because of cumulative transaction costs related to security.[22]

In this pessimistic scenario, the integrity of both public and private security ends up going down the drain because both public and private law enforcement officials begin to see their role as simply vendors of security services in a competitive market, with any distinctions between savory and unsavory clients, reasonable and unreasonable objectives, or civilized and uncivilized rules of behavior vanishing due to their increasing fuzziness within an increasingly unstructured environment in which force is simply a commodity for sale to the highest bidder.

Another worry about privatized security, common to both domestic law enforcement and foreign military assistance, is the possibility of tension between public and private forces. In particular, friction may frequently surface between private security forces and government army or police personnel.[23] The underlying logic here is that government security officials would see the private security providers as superfluous, with inferior qualifications and experience, serving in the end only to interfere with public safety—or makes its enforcement more difficult—rather than to promote it; and private security forces would assume that the whole reason their services were requested was the incompetence, inadequacy, or ineptitude of the public police. There is, for example, a long tradition of military personnel in many countries being more skeptical than others in government about whether nonmilitary people can do the things they do as well as they do. In this way of thinking, expecting these two groups to cooperate harmoniously in pursuit of the common good of national security is rather unrealistic.

In looking at this potential friction between public and private security forces, however, a critical potential for complementary cooperation is being ignored. One U.S. army officer explains how this joint security action could work beneficially for both domestic and international operations:

> Just as private security firms are accepted as a positive development, if successful in reducing crime, so too are military contractors accepted, if successful in assisting an army to accomplish its missions at a reduced cost. Coinciding with the shrinking size of the world's armies is the growing requirements placed upon them. Armies the world over are being asked to perform missions that are outside the traditional mission of defending national sovereignty. Assisting the nation in the policing of national borders, combating drugs, and humanitarian relief missions are now the everyday missions of armies around the world. What had been traditional police missions now have a mix of police, private security firms and military working in the same arena. With the proliferation of private security firms and military contractors who assist the armies, it is time the US Army begins to consider the implications of operating in an environment where the most capable military force may be a private company, not a government entity.[24]

While this enlightened attitude is certainly not the dominant way of thinking among the world's government police and army personnel, it points to potential benefits that are hard to ignore.

As to the other concerns about the impact of security privatization on domestic law enforcement, while in theory privatization would help to "commodify" security and provide incentives for it to be bought and sold indiscriminately, in practice many believe this is simply not the case. In those instances where some domestic law enforcement functions have been privatized, the net result has not generally been the demobilization or demoralization of local government police forces. What has resulted instead has been the increased two-way flow of security personnel between private companies and government agencies, which has in many people's minds increased the mutual understanding and willingness to cooperate of the two sectors. With public-private security burden sharing becoming more common, it appears that the two types of protection providers will have more chances to learn how to work together. There appears to be no inherent reason, given the similarity of training and experience of those who work for public and private security outfits, that a socially responsible and mutually supportive complementary relationship could not emerge here of great benefit to the citizenry at large.

Impact on Foreign-Policy Effectiveness

Turning to the foreign-policy effectiveness of privatized foreign security assistance, a parallel heated debate exists about the international consequences. Some claim employing this means as a foreign-policy tool ends up, at times inadvertently, becoming the equivalent of conducting foreign policy "by proxy," with the long-standing asset of plausible deniability eliminating the possibility of any sustained and coherent link between foreign-policy principles and interventions actually undertaken.[25] Others worry that it makes no sense from a national-security standpoint that military assistance would be in effect for sale on the international marketplace, causing an uncontrolled dissemination of warfighting skills, lethal arms to be viewed as neutral commodities, and a loss of faith in the official military establishment.[26] Still others are fearful that the availability of private military services may attract unhappy insurgent groups or feisty rogue states and used as a tool to foment instability.[27] All of these worries revolve around a belief that somehow accountability, controllability, and restraint diminish or even vanish when private security providers are used as instruments of foreign policy.

In addition to these unintended negative foreign-policy consequences, there are those who fear a more devious—perhaps even conspiratorial—

intentional use of privatized security by national governments for negative foreign-policy ends. Some see private foreign military assistance as
a new form of colonialism, with "mercenaries becoming the shock force
of corporate recolonisation"[28] and home governments explicitly using
private military forces as a subtle way to maintain influence over less
powerful states.[29] In this view, reliance on external private security
providers may generate a debilitating dependency in which "client
states could rely indefinitely on private armies rather than seek a holis-
tic approach to the resolution of their conflicts."[30] In addition, it is conceivable to some that the most unscrupulous private military companies
could have an interest in seeing violence and turmoil perpetuated to
drum up business for their services. In these cases, broad pursuit of the
national interest with the integrity ideally associated with state security
policymakers is presumably replaced by corruption, greed, and a lust
for power.

However, there is another side to this picture. Representatives of
private military companies argue that the integrity of their own staff
prevents abuse of power, that they are careful in choosing clients that
will not use newly acquired capabilities against these firms' home
states, and that in any case the defensive training and advice they give
cannot be readily converted for offensive purposes.[31] It is certainly possible that employing private security forces can accelerate foreign-
policy responsiveness and reduce overseas entanglements. The uncontrolled spread of military capabilities and the conduct of foreign policy
"by proxy" have been and would be occurring even without the presence of private security providers, for example, in the first case, through
illicit government-to-government arms transfers and, in the second case,
through the use of unannounced covert government operations. The
same is certainly true for using foreign policy to attain neocolonialist
ends; if no private security companies existed, other multinational corporations could easily fill the vacuum here. The specter of private military providers promoting widespread international instability (for reasons of profit or political ideology) ignores that their strength in
weaponry and personnel is sufficiently small that the only places where
they have reasonable prospects of achieving these non–status quo goals
are those where turmoil is already rampant. Furthermore, many government officials, such as former deputy assistant secretary of defense for
African affairs James Woods, do believe that privatized security efforts
can help to relieve anarchy and chaos, keep local security disruptions
from spreading, and provide sound defense against outside threat.[32]

Conclusion

The worst-case scenario for the long-term consequences of security privatization includes the destruction of a sense of community obligation and the mass magnification of perceived fear; the creation of a "might-makes-right' social order; the widening of the gap between the rich and the poor; the hollowing out of the state; the proliferation of violence and crimes against humanity; the corruption of coercive authority and the intensification of friction between public and private authorities; and the irresponsible, uncontrolled, and potentially neocolonialist use of foreign-policy influence. Perhaps the most significant finding from this overview of potential consequences of privatized security is how they may serve in many ways to amplify the causes of this phenomenon: the prevalence of panic, inequality, unjust coercion, and state weakness, corruption, or irresponsibility can all both stimulate and result from security privatization. Figure 4.1 summarizes this potentially gloomy picture, typifying the image held of the privatization of security by its worst critics. While in each case there are also equally compelling arguments depicting a much brighter side to the picture, with distinct benefits emerging on the local, national, and global levels, the dire concerns about pernicious consequences mean at the very least that those choosing to utilize privatized security should do so with extreme care. More than anything else, the worries identified in this chapter serve to highlight justified skepticism of universal claims about the benefits of this potent security instrument.

It is thus not just a random rolling of the dice that will ultimately determine whether the privatization of security will lead to the creation of a pernicious or beneficial security picture. The use of private security providers is instead decidedly the product of intentional—if not fully informed—human choice. Even today, without sustained data on the projected outcomes from security privatization, states, groups, and individuals who use them are trying to make sound decisions based on what little evidence they have at their disposal.

The basic problem is that this security instrument is a rather small, short-term, and temporary one compared to many government military operations, and as a result determining with any degree of certainty what the probable outcome from its use might be is extremely difficult even under the best of circumstances. Nonetheless, charting out the full spectrum of projected outcomes, regardless of the level of confidence any one possesses, can make security policy choices about privatization more clear.

Figure 4.1 Worst-Case Security Privatization Consequences

Impact of Privatized Security on Individual Attitudes
• *Selfish Panic*
  Destruction of a Sense of Community Obligation
  Mass Magnification of Perceived Fear

Impact of Privatized Security on Societal Norms
• *Unjust Inequality*
  Creation of a "Might-Makes-Right" Social Order
  Widening the Security Gap Between the Rich and the Poor

Impact of Privatized Security on State Responsibilities
• *Governmental Facade*
  Externalization of State Security Functions
  Loss of State Control over Society

Impact of Privatized Security on Conflict Management
• *Institutional Violence*
  Facilitation of Coercive Force as the Tool of Choice
  Militarization of Government Security Forces

Impact of Privatized Security on Domestic Law Enforcement
• *Vanishing Integrity*
  Corruption of Coercive Authority
  Intensification of Friction Between Public and Private Security
    Officials

Impact of Privatized Security on Foreign Policy
• *Abandoned Restraint*
  Neocolonialist Foreign Policy Influence
  Irresponsible Conduct of Foreign Policy by Proxy

Notes

1. Edward J. Blakely and Mary Gail Snyder, "Places to Hide," *American Demographics* 19 (May 1997): 23–25.

2. Julie Gallagher, "Anti-Social Security," *New Statesman & Society* 8 (March 31, 1995): 22–24.

3. Peter Lock, "Africa, Military Downsizing and the Growth in the Security Industry," in Jakkie Cilliers and Peggy Mason, eds., *Peace, Profit or Plunder? The Privatisation of Security in War-Torn African Societies* (Johannesburg: Institute for Security Studies, 1999): p. 26.

4. Leonard Berkowitz, *The Roots of Aggression* (New York: Atherton Press, 1969).

5. David Shearer, "Outsourcing War," *Foreign Policy* 112 (fall 1998): 75.

6. Owen Greene, "From Mercenaries to Private Security Companies: Options for Future Policy Research," presentation at a Consultation on Private Military Companies held at the International Alert Offices in London on December 8, 1998.

7. Blakely and Snyder, "Places to Hide," p. 25.

8. Lock, "Africa, Military Downsizing" p. 26.

9. International Alert, *The Privatization of Security: Framing a Conflict Prevention and Peacebuilding Policy Agenda* (London: International Alert, April 2001): p. 13.

10. John Harker, "Mercenaries: Private Power, Public Insecurity?" *Life & Peace Institute* (April 1998): http://www.life-peace.org/nroutes/merc498.htm, p. 7.

11. Eboe Hutchful, "Understanding the African Security Crisis," in Abdel-Fatau Musah and J. 'Kayode Fayemi, eds., *Mercenaries: An African Security Dilemma* (London: Pluto Press, 2000): p. 214.

12. Abdel-Fatau Musah and J. 'Kayode Fayemi, eds., *Mercenaries: An African Security Dilemma* (London: Pluto Press, 2000): p. 4.

13. Peter Lock, "Military Downsizing and Growth in the Security Industry in Sub-Saharan Africa": http://www.idsa-india.org/an-dec8-10.html.

14. Captain C. J. van Bergen Thirion, "The Privatisation of Security: A Blessing or a Menace?" 1998: http://www.mil.za/CSANDF/CJSupp/Training-Formation/DefenceCollege/Researchpapers1998/privatisation_of_security.htm.

15. Greene, "From Mercenaries to Private Security Companies."

16. Private Correspondence from Michael Renner, June 3, 1999.

17. "Philippines: Private Armies, Public Enemies," *Economist* 328 (August 14, 1993): p. 34.

18. Funmi Olonisakin, "Mercenaries Fill the Vacuum," *World Today* 54 (May 1998): 146.

19. International Alert, "Use of Mercenaries as a Means of Violating Human Rights and Impeding the Exercise of the Right of Peoples to Self-Determination" (London: unpublished submission to The United Nations Commission on Human Rights, March 26, 1999).

20. Douglas Farah, "Cartel Hires Mercenaries to Train Security Forces," *Washington Post* (November 4, 1997): p. A12.

21. Herbert M. Howe, "Global Order and the Privatization of Security," *Fletcher Forum of World Affairs* 22 (summer/fall 1998): p. 5.

22. Lock, "Military Downsizing and Growth."

23. Howe, "Global Order and the Privatization of Security," p. 4.

24. Major Thomas J. Milton, "The New Mercenaries—Corporate Armies for Hire" (Foreign Area Officer Association, December 1997): http://www.faoa. org/journal/newmerc3.html.

25. Ken Silverstein, "Privatizing War," *The Nation* 265 (July 28–August 4, 1997): 12.

26. Bruce D. Grant, "U.S. Military Expenditure for Sale: Private Military Consultants as a Tool of Foreign Policy," unpublished paper entered in the 1998 Chairman of the Joint Chiefs of Staff Strategy Essay Competition, Institute for National Strategic Studies, 1998.

27. Summary of Proceedings, Defense Intelligence Agency Conference, "The Privatization of Security in Sub-Saharan Africa" (Washington, DC: unpublished document, July 24, 1998): pp. 1–2.

28. Musah and Fayemi, *Mercenaries,* p. 1.

29. Howe, "Global Order and the Privatization of Security," p. 4.

30. Olonisakin, "Mercenaries Fill the Vacuum," p. 146.

31. Interview with Ed Soyster, vice president for operations, MPRI, Alexandria, VA, July 23, 1999.

32. David Isenberg, "Have Lawyer, Accountant, and Guns, Will Fight: The New Post–Cold War Mercenaries," paper presented at the annual national convention of the International Studies Association (Washington, DC: February 19, 1999): p. 9.

5

PRIVATE SECURITY SERVICES:
A TAXONOMY

Prior to further discussion about the privatization of security, it is important to make clearer in light of recent trends what exactly is included and excluded by this topic. A basic premise here is that developing a single all-encompassing definition without any subdivision is futile due to the truly multidimensional nature of privatized security. While many analyses treat privatized security as one unified homogeneous phenomenon, in reality it incorporates a wide variety of divergent yet interrelated patterns. The fundamental concept of nongovernmental provision of security services leaves a lot of ambiguity about what falls under this mantle. Crucial differences in scope, source, form, and function exist, although as with any proposed taxonomy many applications of security privatization cut across categories. This chapter presents a basic definition of private security providers, discusses the prevailing ways of subdividing them, and then chooses a rather novel approach to identifying multiple strands of their activity, rather than artificially attempting to meld all of the forms into a tight unified rubric. Through brief clarification of key distinctions in this chapter, it quickly becomes clear that many sweeping generalizations about privatized security need qualification.

General Operational Definition
of Private Security Providers

At perhaps the most basic level, questions emerge about what kinds of groups the privatization of security identifies. To begin with, this study employs the general label "private security providers" to encompass the broadest range of those generating this kind of service. The concept of security embedded here is a rather basic one, revolving around the physical and psychological safety from danger of those protected. To be considered a private security provider, two criteria need to be satisfied:

1. The ownership and control of the organization providing the services has to be distinctly nongovernmental; and
2. The nature of the services provided has to focus on the provision of coercive security, including such elements as advice, logistical support, intelligence, or direct combat troops and related equipment.

This simple and parsimonious definition appears broad enough to encompass the full range of activities associated with the privatization of security in the modern era.

What is omitted from this definition, however, is as important as what is included. There is no restriction whatsoever on the recipients of private security services, thus allowing for both governmental and nongovernmental beneficiaries. There is no requirement here that private security providers have a minimum size, level of formal organization, or scope of operations (domestically or internationally) to be included, thus allowing for coverage of both disorganized local self-defense forces and formal large-scale global military companies. There is no statement here about whether the private security providers are indigenous or alien with respect to the area in which they operate, thus allowing for coverage of private groups active within their own country as well as someone else's. There is no implication that private security providers are either acting on their own or on behalf of a client—governmental, corporate, or individual—who may or may not be a party to an ongoing conflict, thus encompassing those colluding closely with national and local governments, those serving international, transnational, or subnational organizations, and those out for their own personal idiosyncratic ends (or those of other individuals). There is no need for included organizations to be attempting to be acting in support of the status quo rather than acting to subvert it, thus including armed insurgent groups and criminal extortion gangs as well as those entities working carefully to keep things the way they are. While security services provided must relate in some way to the use of coercion to create or maintain order, there is no specification of the kind of coercion applied and no assumption that incorporated organizations actually undertake any type of coercive action, thus facilitating the inclusion of business-suited security consultants who never venture outside of their offices as well

as combat troops in army fatigues who perform exclusively in the battlefield. There is no underlying premise that participants in the private
provision of security have any particular type of motivation to pursue
this line of work, thus including the full span of personal and corporate
justifications ranging from lust for money to passion for ideology as a
basis for choosing the mercenary vocation. Finally, there is no mandate
that covered groups care in any way, shape, or form about broader societal security, thus permitting incorporation of narrowly oriented gated
communities as well as broad foreign security intervention.

One of these premises seems particularly controversial and in need
of additional elaboration—that private security providers should include
non–status quo outfits as well as those protecting the status quo. Many
would argue that the notion of providing security inherently means attempting to protect people from danger and secure their safety, thus implying that if one's goal is to overthrow or subvert the system then one
cannot be a part of the private security business. The implication from
such a notion would be, for example, that groups attempting coercively
to change a regime, even if it were from an unjust to a just one, would
be intrinsically private security destroyers rather than private security
providers.

However, it is this study's contention that it is extremely important
to integrate coverage of both status quo and non–status quo private security providers, for three reasons. First, both varieties are prevalent in
today's world, and conceptually both types of security privatization are
crucial in understanding the way in which demand for and supply of
private security services work within the current international system.
Second, non–status quo forces included in this study are those seeking
to establish a new protective order to replace the existing one, not those
seeking simply to demolish all protective systems and create an atmosphere of total chaos. Third, it is difficult in today's post–Cold War security environment to differentiate between those coercive groups seeking to preserve the existing distribution of power and those seeking to
overturn it: with many governments possessing dubious internal or external legitimacy, and many ethnic, religious, racial enclaves reinter-
preting the status quo in ways that serve their interests, it is hard to
imagine drawing a clear dividing line between those who want to keep
things the way they are and those who want dramatic change. Just as it
is hard to make a clear demarcation between terrorists (who are considered anti–status quo) and freedom fighters (who are often considered to
be trying to restore a preexisting status quo), so it would be hard to separate conceptually private gangs who provide useful stability-enhancing

protection to a population otherwise in danger and private gangs who victimize and exploit a community by creating an atmosphere of terror and violence.

While this book pays the most attention to analyzing the costs and benefits of more organized, coordinated, and self-regulating private security outfits, it seems impossible to exclude completely the many varieties of subnational and transnational groups who either in principle or in practice do not display an exercise of restraint and strict adherence to mission in carrying out a range of security-oriented activities deemed protective by at least some class of people. Considering formal private security companies without taking account of mercenaries on the international level makes as little sense as considering formal private policing units without taking account of vigilantes and militias on the domestic level. Even today there are almost completely unorganized bands of roving mercenaries motivated strictly by profit, many of which regularly commit massacres, rapes, and looting; these groups deserve inclusion in this analysis despite being completely outside the bounds of normal provision of security needs.[1] For those highly critical of mixing crude mercenary behavior with that of highly reputable private military companies, it is important to keep in mind that even national government military forces in many countries of the world have a decidedly checkered record with regard to undertaking a variety of human-rights abuses in the normal course of executing official orders. Thus, attempting to exclude unsavory private security providers, and incorporate only the truly savory ones, the way many do among both supporters and opponents of security privatization, makes little sense.

Defining private security providers this broadly is virtually unprecedented and poses at least one important obstacle to overcome. Perhaps most generally, the possibility emerges of discussing groups that are so diverse and different in their interests that overarching generalization becomes impossible. This classic "apples-and-oranges" dilemma is certainly a major problem here, as vigilante groups, private military companies, home security outfits, and rogue mercenaries appear at least on the surface to share little in common; but upon closer scrutiny display parallels in sources and impacts, including most particularly the way in which they affect the security or insecurity of governments and their citizens, that end up being truly remarkable. Furthermore, from a policy standpoint, it appears to be rather fruitless and counterproductive to attempt to reign in and restrain one type of coercive protective group while leaving another outside of the defined bounds of sanctioned activity.

Traditional Conceptual Breakdown
of Private Security Providers

In sharp contrast to this book's more inclusive approach, to be presented in the next section of this chapter, most analysts—particularly those focusing exclusively on the international use of private security providers—have subscribed to a much narrower three-part division ranging from, on the scruffy end of the spectrum, mercenaries (ad hoc groups of professional soldiers operating for personal gain), proceeding to private military companies (organized groups providing military services including direct support in combat operations), and ending with private security companies (organized groups providing protection but not engaging in military operations).[2] There are certainly advantages to this kind of categorization scheme, which combines a measure of the degree to which a group is involved in actual fighting with that of the degree to which a group commands societal respect and acceptance. However, it appears that this scheme is neither sufficiently clean in its subdivisions nor sufficiently comprehensive in scope to distinguish clearly among the broad range of privatized security activities this book deems to be important. Indeed, this kind of categorization scheme may be based more on the vagaries of "profit margins and commercial opportunity" than on any overarching substantive conceptual distinctions.[3]

To illustrate the difficulties here, it is worth exploring how the two ends of this three-point spectrum of privatized security activity are customarily defined. On the most formal end of this continuum, private security companies are considered to be those that offer such services as personnel and installation protection, security training, and counter–industrial espionage techniques.[4] They provide "passive security for private and public facilities and operations in high-risk conflict zones."[5] However, it is rather difficult to determine in practice exactly what kinds of firms should be included and excluded here. Moreover, this categorization system would appear in practice to eliminate coverage of those groups seeking non–status quo ends, such as insurgents or gangs, in favor exclusively of those seeking to protect the existing distribution of power.

On the most informal end of the continuum, an individual classified as a mercenary usually has to be someone who:

1. is specifically recruited locally or abroad in order to fight in an armed conflict;

2. does, in fact, take direct part in the hostilities;
3. is motivated to take part in the hostilities essentially by the desire for private gain and, in fact is promised, by or on behalf of a party to the conflict, material compensation substantially in excess of that promised, or paid to combatants of similar ranks and functions in the armed forces of that party;
4. is neither a national of a party to the conflict nor a resident of territory controlled by a party to the conflict;
5. is not a member of the armed forces of a party to the conflict; and
6. has not been sent by a state which is not a party to the conflict on official duty as a member of the armed forces.[6]

The definition of a mercenary has admittedly been a particularly "complex, confusing, emotionally and politically charged issue that official bodies wince at, minor powers fear, and various lobby groups seize as a platform."[7] Like the definition of private security companies on the other end of the spectrum, these criteria provide some useful delineation but serve to omit key groups and leave a large amount of room for subjective interpretation and ambiguity. In particular, the first arbitrary exclusion embedded in this definition is restricting private security providers to those who actually fight in armed conflicts rather than those who provide reconnaissance, military advice, logistical support, intelligence, or combat equipment in a conflict situation. A second unfortunate restriction present here is that only certain motivations—desire for private gain or material compensation—are acceptable, eliminating in the process those private groups who seek to provide security services out of such justifications as civic duty, ideological fervor, or even a pure sense of adventure. A third deficiency is the exclusion of those private military forces who happen to originate in the same country as that where the fighting is taking place, axing coverage of those seeking to help protect or overthrow their homeland political regime. A final element of undue narrowness is the exclusion of those private security providers contracted by states outside of those involved in an ongoing conflict, eliminating for example the possibility of private military forces legitimately requested by allies (unilaterally or multilaterally) to achieve stability abroad.

While less discussion has occurred about how to subdivide explicitly domestic security privatization, it is worth mentioning briefly how this is conventionally accomplished. On the most formal end of this continuum, private security companies can be divided into the following broad categories:

1. The guarding sector, which is by far the largest and most visible component. Regions with the highest levels of crime and private enterprise have the largest number of security companies. These activities range from urban to rural security.

2. The electronic security and hardware sector includes installers of alarms and quick reaction devices, often with reaction services attached.

3. The investigation and risk management sector, which is the smallest and comprises private investigators whose activities include matrimonial disputes, labour matters, industrial espionage, a growing number of criminal investigations and to a lesser extent VIP protection. The collection of risk management consultants is the least visible of all sectors and is the sector which . . . is perceived to be the most problematic and potentially threatening to the state.[8]

Another commonly accepted organizational scheme distinguishes among guard companies, alarm companies, investigation services, computer firewall firms, and Internet security providers.[9] Thus rather than differentiating among the various types of domestic private security providers, as in the case of the conventional international delineation, there is an attempt here to demarcate different services provided. But as with traditional global security schemes, there appears to be both arbitrariness and overlap in drawing this degree of detailed distinctions among functions.

This Study's Conceptual Breakdown of Private Security Providers

Having presented a general notion of privatized security and contrasted it to prevailing methods of subclassification, this book chooses to provide its own subdivision scheme, creating in effect a taxonomy of security privatization. Given that generalizations about all the varieties of private security providers would often prove to be too sweeping, this breaking down of security privatization into subtypes can help to facilitate more modest and meaningful restriction of conclusions. The particular categories chosen for discriminating differing varieties of privatized security are, rather intuitively, the scope, source, form, and function of this phenomenon. Each cluster of types of privatized security inescapably involves simplification of complex sets of distinctions into opposite ends on mono-dimensional continua, and each equally inescapably downplays other possible clusters of types within the same category; nonetheless, despite these limitations, the resulting scheme appears to be useful as a form of conceptual organization for this multifaceted phenomenon. Figure 5.1 summarizes for purposes of clarity the overall taxonomical scheme.

Scope of Privatized Security

Beginning with issues of scope, here is where popular misunderstanding is often greatest. Most of the awareness and discussion centers on privatized foreign security assistance, supplied by nongovernmental sources in one state (often at the request of a government) to either governmental or nongovernmental parties in another state. Either the provider (which tends to be within advanced industrial societies) or the recipient (which tends to be in developing countries) may initiate this assistance. But an equally important pattern, largely ignored by many examining foreign security assistance, occurs when the provider and recipient are within the same country: in many states, both developed and developing, there is a partial replacement of national government police forces responsible for maintaining internal order by privatized security forces composed of people indigenous to that same society. Even when onlookers have become aware of both types of privatized security, they often see no connection between them despite the parallels in their form and function. Of course, situations where foreign security assistance goes to both a national army and a government police force, or where a single private company provides both domestic and foreign security services, serve to cloud this distinction a bit.

The artificial isolation of external from internal security privatization seems odd, despite the general inability of local security firms to provide military training comparable to international private security companies,[10] because the growth of private security services internationally is largely an extension of their more prominent domestic role.[11] Moreover, as more and more countries see the distinction between domestic police and external armies blur due to threats that combine a mix of internal and external origins, domestic and international private security providers are seeing their scope and methods becoming increasingly interconnected. While in the academic world domestic-setting-oriented sociologists focus largely on internal security privatization and international relations scholars focus largely on external security privatization, in the real world the two need parallel and integrated treatment.

Both privatized foreign security assistance and privatized domestic security substitution themselves could of course be further broken down

Figure 5.1   Taxonomy of Security Privatization

Scope of Privatized Security

Foreign Assistance vs. Domestic Substitution

- *Privatized Foreign Security Assistance*
  Nongovernmental sources in one state provide privatized security services to either governmental or nongovernmental parties in another state.

- *Privatized Domestic Security Substitution*
  Privatized security services provided by unofficial individuals or groups indigenous to a given society replace national government police services responsible to maintain internal order.

Source of Privatized Security

Top-Down vs. Bottom-up

- *Privatized Top-Down Security Services*
  Governments outsource their internal or external security functions to private foreign or domestic providers.

- *Privatized Bottom-Up Security Services*
  Individuals or loosely organized societal groups (such as militias, vigilantes, neighborhood watches, self-defense forces, gangs, and survivalists) initiate provision of security services to themselves or to others.

Form of Privatized Security

Direct Combat Support vs. Military Advice

- *Privatized Direct Combat Support*
  Private providers supply either the fighting forces themselves (usually mercenaries or private armies) or the tools of violence (usually small and large conventional weapons systems).

- *Privatized Military Advice*
  Private providers supply classroom education on fighting strategy and tactics or on-site battle training (in neither case are the providers involved in actual combat situations).

Purpose of Privatized Security

Status Quo vs. Non–Status Quo

- *Privatized Status Quo Security Services*
  Recipients obtain private security services so as to keep order, guard against threat, and maintain the existing distribution of power.

- *Privatized Non–Status Quo Security Services*
  Recipients obtain private security services so as to overthrow established sources of authority and power.

into subcategories. For foreign assistance, involving the alien entrance of nongovernmental security help from abroad, Chapter 1's discussion of recent trends showed that key distinctions exist among war-fighting, peacekeeping, humanitarian assistance, investment protection, and intelligence-gathering varieties. However, all of these have the commonality that private security providers are intervening abroad with the end of at least temporarily restoring stability. For domestic substitution, involving the indigenous emergence of nongovernmental security relief from at home, a major divide exists between large formal security companies contracting through established processes to replace police services and small ad hoc informal vigilante groups assuming, given no consultation with others, these same tasks. Yet at the same time some major similarities and overlaps exist in the way both end up augmenting and ultimately relieving a government of internal security responsibilities it often cannot provide as effectively. In other words, the distinctions among different types of privatized foreign security assistance, or among different types of privatized domestic security substitution, do not appear as crucial in identifying distinctive patterns of behavior as does the basic foreign-domestic split.

Source of Privatized Security

Turning to the source of security privatization, the most important issue revolves around whether the privatized security is fundamentally top-down or bottom-up. Often both the legitimacy and effectiveness of an application of security privatization can result directly from the nature of the initiation of its use. It is readily apparent that different parties may be involved in security privatization—governments (though these by definition cannot be direct providers), transnational, international, and subnational not-for-profit organizations, for-profit corporations, and societal groups and individuals. When a government decides to outsource its internal or external security functions to private security providers, either domestic or foreign, that is a top-down initiation of privatized security. When individuals, subnational organizations, or loosely organized societal groups (such as militias, vigilantes, criminals, neighborhood watches, self-defense forces, gangs, or survivalists) decide for themselves to provide their own security or to offer security services to others, that is a bottom-up form of privatized security. When a multinational corporation (or other transnational organization) decides to provide its own security services, or decides to hire a private security firm (again, either from its own home state or from abroad), it is less immediately apparent whether this is top-down or bottom-up.

The implications of the differences in source between top-down and bottom-up security provision are not insignificant. In the top-down case, the private security provider bears little direct responsibility for the nature of its contracted activities, as any concern would logically need to be directed at the government client who defined the mission and tactics to achieve it; whereas in a bottom-up case, there seems to be a much greater chance that the perceived and actual responsibility will lie with the private security provider. Within countries where there is little popular support for a government, or where the citizenry and government are sharply at odds on security issues, this source distinction between top-down and bottom-up patterns can be especially crucial.

Here again the top-down versus bottom-up distinction could easily be further refined. Within top-down security privatization, there might readily be a subdivision between taking one's directives from national governments and intergovernmental organizations such as the United Nations. Within bottom-up security privatization, there might well be a distinction between private security providers servicing individuals and those working for large organized subnational or transnational nongovernmental groups. However, regardless of the exact nature of the organization at the top or at the bottom initiating the request, there appears to be a cross-cutting set of distinctions—both in the eyes of beholders and in the actual implications for clients and providers—between demand that emanates from governments (individually or collectively) and that which does not.

Form of Privatized Security

Moving to the form of the security privatization, the most crucial distinction is between providing direct combat support and providing military advice. Within the category of direct combat support, which is generally considered to be the more intense form of privatized security, a provider may participate directly in military operations by supplying the fighting forces themselves (usually in the form of mercenaries or private armies) and the tools of violence (usually small and large conventional weapons systems). Within the category of military advice, the provider may supply classroom education on fighting strategy and tactics, battlefield training to the designated recipients, or even insight on civil-military relations within democratic systems. Hazy areas in between these two categories include logistics support during battle and restoration of order after a conflict has ended.

Due to its more immediate strategic impact on the balance of military power, it is widely agreed that direct combat support needs to be separated from military advice. While most of the attention in the popular press has focused on direct combat support, the privatized provision of military advice has been much more commonplace in recent years. The crucial issues of perceived internal and external morality and legitimacy hinge heavily (and often arbitrarily) in many cases on whether the private provision of security services involves actual battlefield fighting or just consultation about what might be prudent.

Here again the macrodistinction between direct combat support and military advice glosses over many smaller differentiations that could be made. Within direct combat support, is the private security provider undertaking all of the combat by itself (or the bulk of the fighting), or is it simply assisting a governmental force to accomplish its ends? Is the command and control of field operations in the hands of the private provider or a government? Is the task purely a military one, such as victory on the battlefield, or does it involve restoring order—and maybe even civil discourse—within the civilian elements of society as well? Within the field of military advice, is the private military provider gathering its own intelligence on which to base this advice? Is this provider training the troops that actually do the fighting using equipment or technology that these government troops did not previously have access to? To what extent is a private security provider the only source of such advice (where the private advice turns out to be definitive), compared to one of many sources of advice (where the private advice turns out to be ancillary)? While these questions and subcategories are all important, none overrides the reality that the most important conceptual and operational distinction boils down to simply whether the private security provider is getting directly involved in the violence itself; even in terms of the basic cost of the contract itself, that is often the make-or-break issue.

Purpose of Privatized Security

Finally, turning to the purpose of the privatized security, the most important distinction is between its status quo or non–status quo orientation (attempting to distinguish among motives of individual mercenaries, such as between rowdy marauders and greedy moneygrubbers, seems problematic). Earlier parts of this chapter argued that both status quo and non–status quo types of private security providers warranted coverage in a discussion of the privatization of security, both because of their importance and because of the difficulties of distinguishing between the two. However, these difficulties in conceptual delineation do not mean that in many cases a continuum cannot be identified with more status quo motives on one end and more non–status quo ends on the other. Although in security circles making a clear-cut offensive-defensive divide has become quite difficult (for example, now it is virtually impossible to separate definitively offensive from defensive weapons), differentiating between the related status quo/non–status quo orientation here appears crucial because of the different baggage associated with each in the security privatization context. In particular, many observers make a moral distinction between protecting people and attacking people for money: with defensive tasks constituting the vast majority of what private security companies handle these days, they appear much more palatable to those with these scruples.[12] Even when existing power structures—whether they be governments, multinational corporations, or other influential transnational and subnational organizations—appear to be illegitimate or corrupt in today's complex international environment, there is a significant difference between having private security providers coercively protect what exists or violently attempt to overturn it.

The motive of the recipient, not the provider, is the key to discerning the two orientations. If a recipient obtains private security services with the aim of keeping order, guarding against threat, and maintaining the status quo, then this falls squarely in the defensive category. If, on the other hand, a recipient obtains private security services in order to overthrow an established legitimate government, then this is clearly an offensive application. The gray area in between is quite vast, due in large part to the obfuscation in today's anarchic global environment about what exactly constitutes the status quo: some examples of this muddiness are using private security services to change the military balance in an ongoing conflict, to unseat an illegitimate despot who recently took control of a country by force, or to empower an angry separatist group that rejects the government in power.

As with the other elements in the security privatization taxonomy, here too the distinction between status quo and non–status quo activities can spawn several subdivisions. Most importantly, it is possible to link status quo defensive behavior by a private security provider to concerns by that provider—or its client—about the general societal welfare or about the broad preservation of a belief system; and in contrast to link non–status quo offensive behavior by a private security provider to narrow selfish concerns about its own benefits—economic, political, or cultural—from such action. Furthermore, it is conceivable that a further distinction might be drawn between whether a private security provider's overall mission is status quo or non–status quo versus whether its strategy and tactics during a confrontation are largely one or the other. But although this distinction is admittedly the weakest and most controversial of those presented in this taxonomy, the basic status quo/non–status quo divide appears to be central because it most directly links to a crucial value among great powers in today's world—whether security privatization is in the end more likely to help maintain international stability or destroy it.

Conclusion

This rather extensive taxonomical discussion has attempted to serve not as an idle navel-gazing exercise, but rather to illuminate—and to some degree guide—the analysis that follows. Deviating rather sharply from classifications found in most of the security privatization literature, the conceptual splits presented here aspire to shed greater light on a differentiated understanding of the topic at hand. Of all the divisions identified within this chapter, the one that appears to be most central is the first—that distinguishing privatized foreign security assistance and privatized domestic security substitution. Compared to the other sets of binary classifications, this difference in scope seems to be both the least ambiguous and the one most desperately in need of integrated analysis. Indeed, the importance of this split is underscored by its service as an organizing principle for the case studies presented in the next chapter. Within the broad categories of foreign security assistance and domestic security substitution, the distinctions discussed pertaining to source, form, and function further illuminate broad patterns in the empirical record.

Notes

1. Henry Sanchez, "Why Do States Hire Private Military Companies?": http://library-newark.rutgers.edu/global/sanchex.htm.
2. International Alert, *The Privatization of Security: Framing a Conflict Prevention and Peacebuilding Policy Agenda* (London: International Alert, April 2001): p. 7.

3. Captain C. J. van Bergen Thirion, "The Privatisation of Security: A Blessing or a Menace?" 1998: http://www.mil.za/CSANDF/CJSupp/TrainingFormation/DefenceCollege/Researchpapers1998/privatisation_of_security.htm.

4. Kevin A. O'Brien, "PMCs, Myths and Mercenaries: The Debate on Private Military Companies," *Royal United Service Institute Journal* (February 2000).

5. J. Slabbert, "Privatising Peacekeeping Operations: A Viable Alternative in Africa for Overextended UN Capacity?": http://www.mil.za/CSANDF/CJSupp/TrainingFormationDefenceCollege/Reasearchpapers2000_02/slabbert.htm.

6. Thirion, "The Privatisation of Security."

7. James R. Davies, *Fortune's Warriors, Private Armies, and the New World Order* (Vancouver, BC: Douglas & McIntire, 2000): chap. 3.

8. Thirion, "The Privatisation of Security."

9. Davies, *Fortune's Warriors, Private Armies,* chap. 2.

10. Thomas K. Adams, "The New Mercenaries and the Privatization of Conflict," *Parameters* 19 (summer 1999): 103–116.

11. David Shearer, *Private Armies and Military Intervention* (London: Oxford University Press, International Institute for Strategic Studies Adelphi Paper 316, 1998): p. 24.

12. "Can Anyone Curb Africa's Dogs of War?" *Economist* 350 (January 16, 1999): 41.

6

INTERNATIONAL AND DOMESTIC
SECURITY: CASE STUDIES

Despite the absence of definitive comprehensive evidence on global patterns of security privatization, anecdotal data on some particularly interesting cases abound. Because much information on security privatization is by nature both proprietary and confidential, the empirical findings reported here are inescapably tentative and not necessarily representative of the overall trends, thus serving more as an agenda for future inquiry than as a revelation of existing reality. Nonetheless, the eight post–Cold War cases presented here are intentionally chosen to reflect exceedingly diverse uses of private security providers spread all over the world. In accordance with the taxonomy presented in Chapter 5, this case discussion is divided into two parts, dealing first with recipients of privatized foreign security assistance and then with recipients of privatized domestic security substitution. Within each case, the categories of source, form, and function are clearly identified. Because of this book's conceptual focus and the many exhaustively detailed accounts of privatized security cases elsewhere, the presentation of each example is quite brief, with a focus on understanding its immediate precipitants and broader security implications.

The utility of this chapter is ultimately to flesh out—and in some cases call into question—the broad generalizations presented elsewhere in this volume. Most writings on the privatization of security have the reverse emphasis, where a small amount of conceptual discussion appears simply to provide a context for the primary focus on illuminating juicy stories of dastardly or heroic escapades at home and abroad by private security providers. However, as discussed in the introduction, the concern of this book is explicitly to identify overarching integrative patterns relating to privatized security in the modern world.

Recipients of Privatized Foreign Security Assistance

By far the most widely discussed examples of security privatization concern assistance sent to distant foreign countries to stabilize or transform the dilemmas they face. The providers of this assistance come primarily from the United Kingdom, the United States, France, and Israel, and these states differ markedly in the types of security services offered. The recipients are located in all parts of the Third World, as it is not always the poorest of the developing countries that take advantage of this privatized support from abroad. The wide-ranging cases chosen for inclusion here (which admittedly may be a bit more extreme than much privatized foreign security assistance) occurred or are occurring in Sierra Leone, Papua New Guinea, Colombia, and the former Yugoslavia.

Sierra Leone

Examining first the Sierra Leone case, this transmission of private foreign military assistance takes place within a continent that has received more attention than any other for the significance of privatized security impact (indeed, Angola, Liberia, and the Democratic Republic of Congo have also been recent regional recipients).[1] In May 1995, the government of Sierra Leone contracted with Executive Outcomes, a South Africa–based private military company that provided direct combat support (and officially ceased operations on December 31, 1998), to assist in quelling the rebel movement led by the Revolutionary United Front. Over the four-year war, 1.5 million people in that country had become refugees and over 15,000 had been killed, and the government army was small, hastily recruited, devoid of professional skills, and corrupt.[2] Facing a desperate situation in which the insurgents had cut off the government's last major source of domestic revenue earlier that year, President Valentine Strasser elicited direct combat support from Executive Outcomes, and within months the private company had cleared rebels from the capital, removed rebel troops from the principal diamond-mining areas, trained local self-defense units to replace the government army, and even attracted other foreign investors in the mining industry.[3] This impact is not surprising when one takes into account widespread reports of an "unofficial alliance" between Executive Outcomes and the British-based Branch Energy Company, owned by the Canadian mining company DiamondWorks.[4]

Although fostering short-term stability, this private intervention did not succeed in restoring long-term stability to the country. Indeed, the private security assistance was at least in part responsible for some long-range problems: Sierra Leone became subject to extensive influence from foreign mercenaries and experienced a seemingly endless need for protection.[5] Moreover, while in 1996 Sierra Leone's democratic elections went well, the new government continuing to rely on Executive Outcomes for security; after such dependence ended in February 1997, this new regime was overthrown by a coup the following May.[6] Subsequent efforts by ECOMOG (the Economic Community of West African States Monitoring Group) and United Nations peacekeeping troops to restore order have proved relatively futile. A seemingly endless cycle of turmoil has continued, with the violent campaign of the Revolutionary United Front rebels impeding any effectiveness of the Sierra Leone government. As a top-down effort involving direct privatized combat support in pursuing status quo ends, this contrast between short-range success and long-range failure is remarkable.

Papua New Guinea

In the Papua New Guinea case, private foreign security assistance did not even have a chance to be fully implemented before it had an explosive impact. Since 1989 the country had experienced internal turmoil, with a rebel force (the Bougainville Revolutionary Army) aggressively fighting government troops over secessionist issues revolving around control of a lucrative copper mine in Bougainville. Several thousand soldiers and civilians had died in the conflict, with Amnesty International accusing both sides of atrocities.[7] After Sir Julius Chan became prime minister in 1994, he soon realized that he could not militarily resolve the problem, and so in late January 1997 he initiated a $36 million contract with Sandline International, a London-based private military firm providing direct combat support and procurement assistance, to quell the rebellion.[8] Once this arrangement was made public on February 22, however, there was widespread outrage from the Australian government, which as a major aid provider to Papua New Guinea called the use of mercenaries "totally unacceptable"; from the World Bank, which said it would review its loans because of the mercenaries; and from the citizenry of the country itself.[9] Even more important, Brigadier General Jerry Singirok, chief of the government army, denounced the deal with Sandline and on March 17 called for Prime Minister Chan's resignation.[10] Facing mounting internal and external pressures, he did just that on March 26. Before the Sandline soldiers even fired a shot, forty of them were ejected from the country by the government army, and Lieutenant

Colonel Tim Spicer, head of the Sandline operation, was arrested on the charge of illegally possessing a pistol and ammunition.[11]

Ultimately the incident turned into a source of humiliation on all sides, even though a subsequent judicial inquiry revealed that the contract issued to Sandline was legitimate, that Sandline appropriately complied with its terms, and that corruption was not present.[12] This is a classic case where, regardless of legality, an attempt to maintain power backfired and worsened the internal and external respect for a government feeling itself so desperate that it needed to secretly hire a private security provider, respect for the private provider offering its services in such a tangled situation, and respect for the meaning of its alliance (with Australia) and loan (with the World Bank) arrangements where assumptions about the restraints on state behavior were violated. Although none of these negative impacts was the fault of the way Sandline conducted its operations, this case vividly shows the potential for unintended ripple effects that neither the country client nor the private security provider had considered carefully in advance. As in the Sierra Leone case, a top-down request for direct privatized combat support for status quo ends could not resolve underlying tensions in the long run.

Colombia

Turning to the Colombia case, private foreign security assistance went to the aid of a corporation instead of a government. It is well established that Defence Systems Limited, a United Kingdom–based private military company that provides military training and logistics support, has helped (along with the government army) since 1992 to protect British Petroleum (BP) from guerrilla attacks on its operations in Colombia.[13] Defence Systems Limited has set up a company called Defence Systems Colombia to handle this contract, reportedly worth £1 million.[14] As it turns out, BP operates in Casanare, a remote region near the Venezuelan border that is the stronghold of the National Liberation Army, Colombia's second-largest guerrilla group whose favorite target is oil pipelines.[15] In 1996–1997, BP was a target of numerous accusations of complicity in murder, torture, and intimidation, with its private security forces said to include former army officers with poor human-rights records.[16] More specifically, locals who spoke out claimed that they lived in fear of private paramilitary death squads cleansing the area of perceived troublemakers, with the Colombian army doing nothing to restrain this activity; while BP has not directly instigated this violence, the leaders of protests against BP appear to be singled out for persecution.[17]

In response to these accusations, British Petroleum has "kept its head down" and has made no major effort to defend its reputation, arguing that it is a victim of a smear campaign by the National Liberation Army.[18] Similarly, Defence Systems Limited has argued that it "always acts within the laws of those countries in which it operates" and that its people do not carry arms but rather just provide advice.[19]

Like the case of Sandline in Papua New Guinea, the involvement of Defence Systems Limited in Colombia has served to smear mud on all parties involved. Those with suspicions that multinational corporations such as British Petroleum are not cautious or vigilant in dealing with local populations, or are ruthless in violating the human rights of indigenous populations, see this use of private security forces to protect foreign corporate natural-resource interests as a classic case of insensitive capitalist exploitation. Those with concerns that private security providers follow no established civilized rules in their operations within remote regions of foreign countries, where direct monitoring is difficult, use this case to illustrate mercenaries running wild. Finally, those worried that the Colombian government has become so corrupt or ineffective (due in part to drug-related issues) see this example as proof of a largely failed state with no effective control of what goes on within its boundaries. Again, while none of these pernicious outcomes is necessarily due to anything dramatic directly done by Defence Systems Limited, this occasion served to damage the image of private security provision nonetheless. In this case a more bottom-up (corporate) use of direct privatized combat support for status quo ends encountered obstacles similar to the more top-down (government) uses discussed above.

Former Yugoslavia

Finally, examining the case in the former Yugoslavia, private foreign security assistance has attempted to alter the balance of power and restore a measure of stability. Since Serbia attacked Slovenia and Croatia in June 1991 and Bosnia in April 1992, the region has experienced tremendous turmoil. In March 1994 the Pentagon recommended to the beleaguered Croatian defense minister to seek help from MPRI (Military Professional Resources Incorporated), a U.S.-based private military company providing military training and analysis, and soon afterwards MPRI began advising them on military training and on how to run a military force in a democracy with a civilian-controlled army.[20] This effort came to fruition in August 1995 when, seven months after MPRI began its work, the Croatian army drove the Serbs out of the Krajina region.[21]

Buoyed by this success, in May 1996 MPRI garnered a three-year contract with the Bosnian government to build up its army against the
Serbs. This "train and equip" program involved helping with logistical
structure, personnel management, and military training and is reportedly
worth $400 million, funded in part by Islamic nations including Brunei,
Kuwait, Malaysia, Saudi Arabia, and the United Arab Emirates.[22] Proponents of this MPRI intervention argue that the sooner Bosnia was
able to defend itself, the sooner international troops could leave; but
skeptics respond that increasing Bosnian power may ultimately lead to
increased violence in the region, offensive Bosnian moves to recapture
lost territory, and a breakdown of the cease-fire agreed to under the
1995 Dayton Accords.[23]

Notwithstanding the later turmoil in Kosovo, MPRI claims that its
operations in Bosnia have indeed been effective, measured by both the
absence of significant fighting within Bosnia and the three-time renewal
of MPRI's contract there.[24] However, despite the short-term success,
there are—as was the case with Sierra Leone—serious concerns about
the long-run implications. Few would argue today that, in the absence
of any private or public foreign military presence, the peoples of the
former Yugoslavia would live together harmoniously in peace. Indeed,
the evidence of the last few years has instead indicated that victim eth-
nicities protected by outside forces will choose to take violent revenge
on their former oppressors the moment they get the chance to do so.
While private military providers often pride themselves on only entering conflicts where there is clarity about which side is worthy of support,
in this region it may be impossible to make that determination. Nonetheless, as the only case in the chapter involving privatized military advice rather than direct combat support, this top-down use of privatized
military advice for status quo ends displayed significant promise.

Overall Patterns—
Privatized Foreign Security Assistance Recipients

In reviewing these examples of privatized foreign security assistance,
the military proficiency of the private security providers involved in
managing the tasks assigned is not at issue, but questions do emerge
about the broader implications. In some cases, such as in Sierra Leone
and the former Yugoslavia, the initial impact was clearly stabilizing, but
there has been significant reason to worry that after the departure of foreign privatized military assistance chaos will return; while this pattern
is certainly typical of governmental military assistance programs as

well, one could certainly hope for more from privatized security (even in cases where they warn governments about the consequences of their departure). The demonstrated or alleged links between private military companies and mining and drilling interests in the Sierra Leone, Papua New Guinea, and Colombia cases provoke inquiry about whether privatized security ultimately serves either government interests or those of the society as a whole in recipient countries, with extraction of precious natural resources in these cases being a source of continued tension within these societies even outside of the private security issue. The accusations about human-rights violations in the Colombia case, and the internal and external outrage in response to security privatization in the Papua New Guinea case, show that many private security providers continue to suffer from severe image problems regardless of the level of appropriateness of their actual behavior.

Recipients of Privatized
Domestic Security Substitution

Most discussions of the global privatization of security either omit or downplay those circumstances when the decision is made within nations to replace part of one's own government security services with private security services. This type of behavior occurs within a wide range of both advanced industrial and developing countries, and can take a variety of forms ranging from large private armies to small groups of security guards. The cases included here occurred or are occurring in the United States, the United Kingdom, South Africa, and the Philippines.

United States

Looking first at the U.S. case, the most powerful nation in the world has witnessed in recent years the erosion of governmental control over its internal security. The statistics are indeed jarring: $52 billion was spent in 1990 on private security compared to $30 billion on public police; there are today more than 10,000 security companies employing 1.5 million guards, over triple the 554,000 state and local police officers; and "the more than 100,000 gun-toting private guards have more firepower than the combined police forces of the nation's thirty largest urban centers." [25] This past decade has seen an incredible explosion of private security in many forms, including private corporate-run prisons, security guards protecting businesses and personal property, and rent-a-cops maintaining urban order. Gated communities, often involving armed patrols and electric fencing, are perhaps the most visible and intrusive sign of this trend. This particular form of privatization began to spread dramatically in the 1980s to the point where in 1997 there were 20,000 such residential areas composed of more than 3 million units, and many of these are "security zone" communities in which bottom-up efforts by residents (not top-down efforts by local governments or developers) end up closing off access to neighborhoods.[26] Even on an individual level, the purchase of home security systems, most notably provided by Brink's Home Security, has achieved unparalleled popularity (doubtlessly fueled both by growing affluence in certain locales and concerns about vulnerability). Whatever the form of domestic privatized security, these alarming trends are triggered by mass fear of violence and crime combined with diminishing confidence in the ability of government security forces to manage the dangers properly. While in reality the national violent crime rates actually dropped in the late 1980s and early 1990s, media exposure and the unpredictability of perpetrators have kept the U.S. public in an apprehensive state of mind.[27]

Despite providing a tangible sense of increased security for those protected, however, privatized domestic security generates some long-term problems. First, the private security industry is largely unregulated and often hires poorly trained and inadequately screened guards who have in numerous instances engaged in unwarranted violence or shady dealings themselves.[28] The concerns surrounding this issue have led, for example, to heated discussions in the aftermath of the terrorist attack on the United States on September 11, 2001, about whether airport security should continue to be farmed out to private security providers or "federalized" in the public sector. Second, private security enclaves may lead to internal and external conflict, and even racial tensions, without any convincing demonstration of effectiveness in terms of significant crime reduction or closeness of community.[29] Third, those unable to afford private security providers, but who live close to those who do have such private protection in place, may indeed witness an increase in their exposure to violence, thus widening the security gap between the rich and the poor in a country that places at least a rhetorical premium on equality of opportunity.

It is indeed instructive to note that, in the wealthiest country in the world, citizens are not willing to devote adequate monies (through taxes) to protection by the public police and instead end up paying far more to employ private security systems that may be inefficient and even redundant from a community-wide perspective. Such a predicament clearly warrants a focused reassessment by both the federal, state, and local governments as well as the mass public itself. Thus this case of bottom-up use of privatized security for what approximates direct combat support for status quo ends is fraught with problems.

United Kingdom

Moving to the United Kingdom case, the pattern is equally unnerving. In Great Britain, as with the United States, the private security industry is larger than the government's police force, with 7,850 private security firms in the United Kingdom employing more than 162,000 people, compared to 142,000 public police.[30] The roles of these private police are multifaceted, including walking the streets, monitoring public demonstrations, escorting prisoners, and guarding government buildings; and the British government—playing a more promotional role than any of the other governments in the internal security cases discussed here—wants to assign even more tasks to them.[31]

The problem is that these private forces in England are often "unregulated, unaccountable, badly trained, and full of crooks," inducing a more than occasional sense of fear among those supposedly protected, mass confusion about the boundaries of responsibility between the private and public police, and friction between the police and private security companies.[32] A more deeply rooted concern is that the British private security industry responds only to client-driven responsibilities and is regulated only by market forces, in contrast to public police who bear "a national responsibility to society at large."[33] What with the British government Foreign Office notorious for promoting the use of its "flourishing" mercenary business and private security companies for "politically dodgy" foreign missions,[34] its simultaneous move toward the privatization of its domestic police force reinforces an image of a country—whose economy has been slipping as well—losing its grip on both internal and external law and order.

The persistently unanswered question remains as to why the British government deems the country's government police force as being so much less cost-effective than indigenous private security providers. The long-term implications of a significant contraction in government provision of security by a major power remain to be seen, but it is hard to imagine that the prestige of the state would be enhanced in the process. With the spread of domestic security substitution in Great Britain a function of a mix of top-down and bottom-up initiatives, it is interesting to note that the legitimacy and effectiveness of this direct combat status quo effort is not substantially different from the more heavily bottom-up initiatives within the United States.

South Africa

In the case of South Africa, it is indeed ironic that a country that finally has shed its racist apartheid regime has become heavily dependent on privatized domestic security. The scope of this effort is huge, with South African private security firms employing 130,000 guards earning almost $1.5 billion in 1997, more than three times as much as in 1990.[35] There are now ten times more private police than public police in South Africa.[36] Under apartheid, the public police "protected whites and oppressed blacks"; but now, "whites no longer feel safe, and blacks want a proper police service"; both are now disappointed in what the government can provide and do not trust the police to maintain law and order.[37] The reasons the governmental police cannot do the job include low pay, widespread corruption, more restricted police powers, and frictions between veterans of the old apartheid police and new recruits from the African National Congress's old guerrilla army.[38] As a result, private security guards are ubiquitous, watching cars for shoppers, patrolling malls, keeping banks and mining houses safe, and guarding houses and neighborhoods (South Africa has a rough equivalent of gated communities—as do many parts of the world—with guarded streets and apartment blocks).[39] In addition to these private security guards, vigilante groups have emerged and taken law and order issues into their own hands to combat widespread murder, rape, and burglary.

As one could readily imagine, in a country still recovering from the postapartheid transition this heavy reliance on privatized domestic security has decidedly mixed results. Although crime has decreased, the private security forces do not all have proper training (and have been accused of irregular behavior), and the private protection is not affordable to many of those who most need it.[40] The net result can be large security inequalities between the rich and the poor, a tangible slap in the face to those hoping for significant changes to result from the end to racial discrimination. It has to be a source of embarrassment to the Mandela regime that South Africa is second only to Great Britain as a source of mercenary activity, domestic and foreign.[41] In the long run, the ability of the South African government to chart the security course for the country has to be severely impaired by the scope and significance of private security operating within its borders. Remarkably parallel to the use of privatized security within the United States, the bottom-up use of direct combat support for status quo ends in South Africa has guaranteed safety in isolated geographical pockets but not fostered a sense of overall cohesive stability.

Philippines

Concluding with the Philippines case, the emergence of private domestic security forces here has been bottom-up but not in response to demand from the mass public. Private armies—usually paid by powerful local politicians and wealthy provincial landowners in a tradition lasting for centuries—have controlled what goes on in much of the country, with 562 armed groups (ranging in size from a few individuals to units of 300) involving 24,000 men possessing around 11,000 weapons.[42] The largest security force in the Philippines is neither the 102,000-person national police nor the 120,000-person national army, but rather the 182,000 private security guards who are "virtually an army for hire,"[43] with local bosses' private armies clearly better equipped than government forces in some provinces.[44]

With 228,000 licensed and unlicensed firearms present in the country, and lax controls on the books easily overcome by bribes,[45] the potential for anarchic coercion and violence seems huge. Indeed, a government official declared that "political warlords and their thugs have been responsible for some of the most gruesome and heinous crimes in the annals of our society."[46] Despite recent attempts by the Philippine government to rein in this private military activity, it continues even today, with gangs of heavily armed men roaming the countryside for economic gain.[47]

This case is particularly interesting because, while Third World countries are traditionally the recipients rather than the providers of privatized foreign security assistance, many have privately hired military forces for use by the rich and powerful as domestic security substitutes; when this pattern occurs within societies lacking a preexisting tradition of a strong government security structure, the likelihood seems to increase that the application of force will be arbitrary and capricious. In the long run, with corruption hitting both public and private internal security forces, any remnant of the notion of common security guaranteed by the state for all of its citizenry runs the risk of vanishing completely. While some might argue that such an ideal security outcome was never realistic for countries such as the Philippines, the overwhelming entrance of privatized security on the domestic level would seem to make actualization of this state of affairs even more remote. Of all the cases discussed in this chapter, the Philippines is alone in dealing with bottom-up direct combat support for largely non–status quo ends, as the private armies attempt to establish their own rule replacing governmental authority; the result is that issues of justice and fair treatment seem to rise to the surface even more acutely than in the more status quo applications of privatized security.

Overall Patterns— Privatized Domestic Security Substitution Recipients

In looking back at these cases of privatized domestic security substitution, it is clear that part of the citizenry feels a lot safer with this kind of protection—as with foreign security assistance, coercive effectiveness is not seriously in question—but again wider questions surface. All of the examples raise concerns about the integrity of private domestic security forces, and this appears to be a much more serious problem here, due to the lack of enforced rigorous standards imposed by domestic private security providers, than with the major outfits involved in privatized international military assistance. The U.S., British, and South African cases highlight the possibility that privatized domestic security may exacerbate tensions between those protected and those unprotected, or between public and private police forces. The Philippines case provides two broad and interesting security lessons: it illustrates how the government can easily see the spread of private domestic security forces as threatening to the stability of the country as a whole; and it shows how government failure in an attempt to reign in such private security activity can produce a self-fulfilling prophesy in which this failure itself spurs on an escalation of privatized security because of the now supposedly clear inability of the government to manage problems on its own. In the end, all these domestic security substitution cases show how individual and group feelings of increased protection through privatized security can serve at the same time to weaken any real sense of overarching society-wide or state security.

Conditions When Privatized Security Is Most Beneficial or Detrimental

From the preceding case analyses, combined with insights from the earlier more general discussion of causes and consequences, some highly speculative patterns emerge about the circumstances when security privatization is most and least useful at the local, national, and international levels. Given the absence of comprehensive and systematic empirical analysis of data, and the limited consideration of only eight cases in this chapter, this very preliminary exposition is just a first step in moving away from descriptive discussions of the privatized security problem toward a more analytical, conditional assessment of its costs and benefits. Figure 6.1 presents a set of emerging hypotheses about when security privatization appears to be most and least dangerous.

Three clusters of interrelated conditions seem important in assessing when private security providers are most detrimental and beneficial. Specifically, the presence or absence of limited anarchy, political legitimacy, and regional deterrence appear to be most central in determining how these providers associate with what this study deems to be the most important security outcome—political stability or instability. The irony here is that many of the conditions where privatized security may be the most problematic are precisely those where many global clients believe that security privatization appears most essential to establishing internal or external law and order.

The presence or absence of limited anarchy in the expression of violence is a cornerstone condition here. If private security forces operate within a totally anarchic environment, failed state, or area full of unrestrained violence and devoid of the most rudimentary elements of civil society, then the authority vacuum would almost assuredly create a situation where these private forces would fail to establish stability and could even make matters worse. Severe but decidedly limited violent chaos seems to be a crucial prerequisite for the success of private security providers, as "their primary utility is in the long-running small wars—conflicts characterized by lightly armed and marginally trained combatants who are more interested in killing civilians than their military rivals."[48] For example, if a few gangs or rebels engage in violence beyond normal state capacity to restrain, both the governments and the affected populations may be well served by augmenting their protection with private security providers; and if small-scale intractable internal conflicts erupt, utilizing such private forces appears to have a decent chance of inducing a cease-fire and permitting an end to mutual hostilities long enough for diplomatic negotiations to ensue.

A government employing private security providers needs to have its own house sufficiently in order to monitor whether or not such use is serving its ends, because otherwise the use of privatized security forces can easily go haywire. Similarly, most discerning state governments would not want to employ private security providers when dealing with missions involving delicate political sensitivity or requiring the use of highly classified information or material. In such situations, the

Figure 6.1   Hypotheses About Security Privatization Dangers

- *Limited Anarchy*
  Privatized security efforts appear to be more dangerous in international relations when involving attempts to manage rampant violent chaos than limited turmoil.

  Private security efforts appear to be most dangerous in international relations when involving delicate political sensitivity requiring the use of highly classified information than when no such sensitivity exists.

- *Political Legitimacy*
  Privatized security efforts appear to be more dangerous in international relations when involving direct combat support than when involving military advice.

  Privatized security efforts appear to be more dangerous in international relations when involving foreign security assistance than when involving domestic security substitution.

  Privatized security efforts appear to be more dangerous in international relations when involving bottom-up initiation than when involving top-down initiation.

  Privatized security efforts appear to be more dangerous in international relations when involving non–status quo rather than status quo motivations and goals.

  Privatized security efforts appear to be more dangerous in international relations when involving the presence of severe and enduring tensions among deep-seated ethnic, religious, or racial enclaves than when these tensions are absent.

  Private security efforts appear to be more dangerous in international relations when involving providers lacking tight self-monitoring restraint than when involving those with such restraint.

- *Regional Deterrence*
  Privatized security efforts appear to be more dangerous in international relations when involving greater (rather than smaller or equal) private-provider power than that of the host or neighboring governments.

  Privatized security efforts appear to be more dangerous in international relations when involving an unstable (rather than stable) political or social environment surrounding the zone of privatized security activity.

dissemination of sensitive material to the wrong parties—often triggered by unlimited anarchy—could cause regional shock waves.

The presence or absence of political legitimacy also plays an absolutely vital role in determining the desirability of privatized security, although legitimacy and effectiveness do not always go hand in hand here: for example, private security providers protecting a humanitarian relief effort may possess greater legitimacy but not necessarily greater effectiveness than those protecting multinational corporations. If the private military activity disproportionately focuses on areas dominated by particular ethnic, religious, or racial minority groups within a divided country, perceived illegitimacy right from the outset and consequent instability afterwards seem quite probable. Special problems may emerge when asymmetries exist between the boundaries of privately protected security zones and those of contending social enclaves, or alternatively when privatized protection for each enclave is unequal.

Similarly, if private security providers enter a situation due to a request from nongovernmental elements within a society (bottom-up), international legitimacy may be considerably lower than if duly elected state governments (top-down) make the request. An obvious exception here is where civil and orderly subnational groups decide to initiate their own privatized protection in harmony with the goals and values of the state and society as a whole. On the other hand, if private security providers are composed of elements external to the society (foreign security assistance), the activities of such providers in most states may possess far less legitimacy than if indigenous elements constituted this help because of the basic principle of self-determination of peoples. The legitimacy of providing privatized security at home is usually considerably higher than sending it abroad, so much so that sanctioning by the international community may not be necessary for success; but an exception to this pattern is the frequent desirability of impartial outside forces to create peace during a civil war.

In a related manner, due largely to greater support from the international community for long-established regimes, private security providers that prop up the status quo generally gain much more acceptance—and are usually more effective—than those seeking to overturn it. The exception here is, of course, if international sympathy turned toward an oppressed internal group seeking its autonomy from a regime presumed to be corrupt, inept, or evil. Furthermore, private security providers that "limit themselves to services such as training, or supplying equipment or arms to contracting governments or international organizations" are most commonly more successful than those "which seek to offer war-fighting services,"[49] at least in part because of the greater perceived legitimacy of providing advice behind the scenes than engaging directly in fighting and killing combatants. In a related way, private security providers that attempt to keep the peace generally seem more legitimate and effective than those attempting to win wars. Lastly, private security providers with a reputation and track record for tight self-monitoring restraint possess more legitimacy (and more often than not display more effectiveness) than those associated with wild and uncontrolled behavior. This last condition relates indirectly to the relative utility in today's world of those commonly labeled mercenaries and private military companies.

Finally, the presence or absence of regional deterrence is relevant in understanding the utility of privatized security. If a private force entering an area is much more powerful than any of the government forces in that region, then official monitoring and restriction of private military activity becomes highly difficult if not downright impossible, and the specter of an out-of-control destabilizing loose cannon rises to the surface. Similarly, if regional instability surrounds the zone of private security activity—reflecting the breakdown of external deterrence—then even if order is restored within the country in which private providers are operating, this success may be to little avail due to vulnerability to disruptive forces from its neighbors.

Perhaps most obviously, privatized security seems less useful when it is redundant and superfluous. The nongovernmental provision of security as a tool of foreign intervention is problematic not only when occurring in countries where the level of militarization and violence has reached truly overwhelming levels, but also when target states already have effective governance.[50] Similarly, utilizing private security forces to replace domestic police makes no sense when a competent and effective public police force already exists. While some have argued that the efficiency benefits alone of privatized security merit its introduction in already completely secure states, this contention is controversial; it must be admitted, however, that the aforementioned prevalence of paralyzed Western states and dysfunctional Third World states with regard to the current crop of security challenges has worked instead in the direction of making privatized security a virtually nonsubstitutable security instrument.

Conclusion

It is clear from the preceding cases that the global spread of privatized security has had a wide range of implications difficult to summarize under a single rubric. All of the cases directly or indirectly raise questions about the ties connecting private security providers with rich or powerful elements of societies without any incentive to care about those less fortunate. Other concerns highlighted by these applications of privatized security include continuing turmoil despite the entrance of privatized security, embarrassment from failure, suspicions of unscrupulousness and corruption, and ultimately a counterproductive weakening of the state's ability to govern. None of the cases presents an example of unqualified success or failure from the use of security privatization, or points to a singular remedy to resolve the kinds of dilemmas encountered; instead, these examples demonstrate a complex mix of costs and benefits requiring careful hiring decisions by potential clients.

Notes

1. Marcus Mabry, "Soldiers of Misfortune," *Newsweek* 129 (February 24, 1997): 40–41.

2. Herbert M. Howe, "Private Security Forces and African Stability: The Case of Executive Outcomes," *Journal of Modern African Studies* 36 (1998): 313–314.

3. William Reno, "Privatizing War in Sierra Leone," *Current History* 96 (May 1997): 228–229.

4. Kevin Whitelaw, "Have Gun, Will Prop Up Regime," *U.S. News & World Report* 122 (January 20, 1997): 47.

5. Reno, "Privatizing War in Sierra Leone," pp. 229–230.

6. Kevin O'Brien, "Freelance Forces: Exploiters of Old or New-Age Peacebrokers?" *Jane's Intelligence Review* 10 (August 1998): 43.

7. "Papua New Guinea: Executive Incomers," *Economist* 342 (March 1, 1997): 40.

8. Keith Suter, "Mercenaries, Mines and Mistakes," *World Today* 53 (November 1997): 278.

9. Ibid.

10. "Papua New Guinea: Line in the Sand," *Economist* 342 (March 29, 1997): 45.

11. Ibid., pp. 44–45.

12. David Isenberg, "Have Lawyer, Accountant, and Guns, Will Fight: The New Post–Cold War Mercenaries," paper presented at the annual national convention of the International Studies Association (Washington, DC: February 19, 1999): pp. 5–6.

13. O'Brien, "Freelance Forces," p. 44.

14. *BP's Secret Soldiers* (Washington, DC: Center for Defense Information, June 1997): http://www.cdi.org/armstradedatabase/CONTROL/Small_Arms/Mercenaries/BP's_Secret_Soldiers.txt.

15. "Colombia: BP at War," *Economist* 344 (July 19, 1997): 33.

16. Ibid.

17. *BP's Secret Soldiers*, p. 3.

18. "Colombia: BP at War," p. 34.

19. *BP's Secret Soldiers,* pp. 9–10.

20. David Isenberg, *Soldiers of Fortune Ltd.: A Profile of Today's Private Sector Corporate Mercenary Firms* (Washington, DC: Center for Defense Information Monograph, November 1997): p. 15.

21. Mark Thompson, "Generals for Hire," *Time* 147 (January 15, 1996): 35.

22. Isenberg, *Soldiers of Fortune Ltd.,* p. 15; O'Brien, "Freelance Forces," p. 44.

23. Isenberg, *Soldiers of Fortune Ltd.,* p. 15.

24. Interview with Ed Soyster, vice president for operations, MPRI, Alexandria, VA, July 21, 1999.

25. Mike Zielinski, "Armed and Dangerous: Private Police on the March," *Covert Action Quarterly:* http://www,caq.com/CAQ54p.police.html: pp. 1–3.

26. Edward J. Blakely and Mary Gail Snyder, *Fortress America: Gated Communities in the United States* (Washington, DC: Brookings Institution, 1997): pp. 1–11, 99–101.

27. Ibid., p. 100; Zielinski, "Armed and Dangerous," p. 3.

28. Zielinski, "Armed and Dangerous," pp. 3–9.

29. Blakely and Snyder, *Fortress America,* pp. 120–121; and Edward J. Blakely and Mary Gail Snyder, "Places to Hide," *American Demographics* 19 (May 1997): 23–25.

30. Julie Gallagher, "Anti-Social Security," *New Statesman & Society* 8 (March 31, 1995): 23.

31. Ibid., pp. 22–23.

32. Ibid.

33. Ibid., p. 24.

34. Issa A. Mansaray, "Mercenaries: Messiahs of Terror," *Expo Times* (Freetown) (June 8, 2001).

35. "Behind the Razor Wire," *Economist* 350 (January 16, 1999): 42.

36. Herbert M. Howe, "Global Order and the Privatization of Security," *Fletcher Forum of World Affairs* 22 (summer–fall 1998): 8.

37. "Behind the Razor Wire," p. 42.

38. Ibid.

39. Ibid.

40. Ibid.

41. Mansaray, "Mercenaries."

42. Rigoberto Tiglao, "Philippines: Safety Catch," *Far Eastern Economic Review* 156 (September 16, 1993): 26; "Philippines: Private Armies, Public Enemies," *Economist* 328 (August 14, 1993): 34.

43. "Philippines: Safety Catch," p. 26.

44. Donald Goertzen, "Muzzling Illicit Guns," *Far Eastern Economic Review* 153 (July 25, 1991): 35.

45. "Philippines: Safety Catch," p. 26.

46. "Philippines: Private Armies, Public Enemies," p. 34.

47. "Philippines: Separatists and Warlords," *Economist* 350 (February 6, 1999): 44.

48. Doug Brooks, Private Correspondence, June 4, 2001.

49. Kim Richard Nossal, "Bulls to Bears: The Privatization of War in the 1990s": http://www.onwar.org/warandmoney/pdfs/nossal.pdf.

50. International Alert, *The Privatization of Security,* p. 7.

7

COMPLEXITIES SURROUNDING PRIVATIZATION

The founding liberal principles of our open globalized system presume that a state monopoly on violence would be dangerous and that the blooming of competitive private-protection initiatives should be beneficial. In contrast, the underlying realist basis of state sovereignty has consistently had governments maintain the preponderance of coercive force so as to keep order and protect the citizenry against divisive privately initiated turmoil. The fundamental contradiction between these two major schools of thought in international relations helps to explain the sea of complexity surrounding any attempt to apply policy management tools to security privatization. Without intending to belabor this clash or create a sense of overall paralysis among both scholars and policymakers concerned with this issue, this chapter provides an overview of this complexity, discussing the definitional morass (touched upon in the taxonomy) that demonstrates the absence of international consensus; the confused and ambiguous ability to judge the overall impact of privatization on global peace and security; the morality and legitimacy questions that surface due to differing values; and the muddled choices and downright confusion facing policymakers, causing them to be ambivalent about tackling the security privatization issue.

Definitional Morass

Perhaps the primary obstacle to forward progress on the management of the privatization of security is the definitional morass. Despite this book's attempt to create an overarching taxonomy, analysts from all vantage points agree that "there are, as yet, no common definitions, standards and methodologies that can be used" to delineate the boundaries of the phenomenon being discussed.[1] In other words, regardless of whether it is hypothetically possible to come up with workable ways to delineate this phenomenon, until the relevant parties can actually reach agreement about what kinds of mercenaries, private military companies, armed insurgent groups, private vigilantes, and the like—and what kinds of activities by these groups—ought to be subject to concerted scrutiny, progress in developing regulatory policies is not going to get very far.

Furthermore, there is difficulty deciding whether the motivation for private military activity is the pivotal element in determining its acceptability and, if so, what the actual motives are in each case. It is worth noting, for example, that "several countries have laws which forbid fighting for other countries' rebels for profit, but proving such a motive is all but impossible."[2] Because motivation is so difficult to gauge, it appears to be dysfunctional as a central discriminating characteristic.

A key element in this definitional morass revolves around delineating the notion of security itself. In its original form, after the formation of the nation-state system, pursuing security meant protecting a regime and its control of its territory, not protecting the rights of the citizenry living within its boundaries.[3] As time has passed, the notion of what exactly is being protected has become quite murky.[4] While it may be common for private security providers to afford better means than governments of protecting the mass public, it is perhaps more rare for such providers to be superior to government forces in ensuring the long-term continuity of the regime itself. Indeed, one of the ironies surrounding the increased use by national governments of privatized security to promote their own survival is that, for weak or failing states, the very act of turning to private military forces—particularly when they come from other countries—may be an unambiguous step toward the elimination of state control of the society in question.

The blurring of other conceptual distinctions within the security policy realm has also more indirectly impeded initial steps toward the management of security privatization. Affected areas include delineating one society from another by choosing the most meaningful cross-unit boundaries; isolating defense policy from other concerns; interpreting the international power hierarchy by distinguishing between important and unimportant parties; and identifying aggressive action by discriminating between legitimate and illegitimate international behavior.[5] The net result has been that national governmental security policy is often either too cautious or too reckless and that the rationality of strategic debate has decreased. For either governments or the private security providers themselves to decide when it is proper to utilize the private provision of protection would similarly be considerably more difficult with these kinds of ambiguities present, as these companies would not be able to easily escape from the same kinds of muddy distinctions governments confront in their use of public military forces.

Confused Impact on Peace and Security

In order to move forward in the direction of monitoring and regulating private security developments, as suggested by the conditional discussion at the end of Chapter 6, there needs to be far more definitive understanding than exists today about when private security vendors have a net positive or negative impact on peace and security in international relations. As it is now, what with the variety of types and levels of privatized protection, "whether they enhance or detract from 'security' depends on who is doing the reckoning."[6] One example of this subjective pattern is that those living within a heavily fortified area may feel secure even though they are surrounded by a multitude of threats in a chaotic setting. A second instance of arbitrary judgment occurs when private military companies enter an area and after reducing rampant violence expand into other business interests and gain private security contracts, mining rights, and a multitude of nonmilitary business opportunities: while some might consider such privatized activity stabilizing, others conclude that "such action could readily be exploitative and inhibit rather than assist economic competition, local economic opportunity and therefore development."[7] In truth, in several analysts' opinion "it even remains to be seen whether it really is cost-effective in the long run for a company or for a government to buy private protection if the social causes of instability are not being addressed."[8]

Even in the United States, debates continue to rage about the value of privatized security:

> It is not clear that outsourcing of military training saves the U.S. government any money . . . Studies of privatization have found that cost savings depend on competition . . . There is often collusion among competing firms, and long-term contracts lead to opportunistic behavior, such as firms bidding low, knowing that they can add on later. Further, the calculated costs of outsourcing rarely take into account the fact that the Pentagon must hire people to police the contractors.[9]

The cost-effectiveness of the U.S. government outsourcing tasks to private security providers is thus inconclusive, as in some cases it saved the government money and in other cases it did not or actually wound up costing more.

All we have so far is anecdotal evidence and firsthand impressions, which often lack impartiality, "as the impact of private security companies on conflict situations is hard to quantify."[10] An example of such low-credibility off-the-cuff remarks are charges by the United Nations' Special Rapporteur on the Use of Mercenaries that "the presence of mercenaries in armed conflicts tends to make them longer-lasting, more serious, and bloodier"[11]; no systematic study has ever been undertaken to justify such a conclusion. The opportunity costs of turning to private security outfits also desperately need focused assessment, including a comparison of their utility to alternatives such as international or regional governmental peacekeeping operations as well as other forms of transnational private intervention.

Such an assessment of private security operating during conflict may in the end boil down to "the lesser of two evils—either running the risk of total state collapse and anarchy against a background of international indifference, or using private actors who have access to the means of coercion in order to halt additional suffering."[12] When dealing with foreign security assistance in particular, further investigation is needed about whether private security companies can transcend their short-term mode, where a temporary cessation of hostilities occurs as long as armed private peacekeepers are present, to ensure long-term peace and stability within a region.[13] How privatized security fits into the overall conflict-management puzzle remains a mystery.

The Morality Question

Underneath the widespread antagonism toward the privatization of security lies a deep-seated moral revulsion about the prospects of putting public safety in the hands of those working simply for profit. Whether rational or not, the depth of this moral reaction cannot be understated: "For all this, and perhaps justifiably, there is a powerful ground swell of opinion against using hired guns to fight wars and kill people. The abhorrence of employing freelancers to do military work is almost universal. Also, it goes against a fundamental ethos of traditional professional armies."[14] Few privatization trends are more ethically volatile than the extraordinary growth of private security providers; despite the corporate-executive image that these groups are at pains to provide, difficult ethical, moral, and even pragmatic questions remain unanswered.[15]

The idea of paying people to fight and kill in predicaments in which they have no interest raises many hackles. While "a variety of actors in conflicts may be influenced by the prospect of monetary gain," the hostile reactions emerging seem to result more because "private entities are paid to become involved in conflicts that are alien to them and in which they have little stake in the political outcome."[16] In addition, accusations that some private security providers use "people with track records of human rights abuse" indicate a distinct indifference to international moral norms.[17] This indifference may extend to issues such as who is killed during private security operations; for example, there have been reports that private armies providing foreign security assistance have often killed innocent civilians "mistaken as rebels or 'rebel sympathizers'" and have been indiscriminately willing "to 'eliminate' enemies of states."[18] The underlying assumption is that private soldiers' integrity vanishes under such circumstances.

Some onlookers, however, see the moral perspective quite differently. Many moral philosophers recognize that "it is no easy matter to distinguish on moral grounds between mercenarism as a professional activity and the activities of national armed forces."[19] Moreover, there appears to be substantial moral inconsistency between the loud protests about using mercenaries in private foreign security assistance and the relative silence—and tacit acceptance—about using private security firms as domestic substitutes for government police forces.[20] Significant moral advantages may derive from the use of private military companies, as "it may be rational to prefer the mercenary system if only to avoid transforming the general citizenry into the potential agents of total war."[21] Most cynically,

> the contemporary abhorrence of mercenarism reflects not so much a well-founded moral disgust, even (for the most part) prudential good sense; instead it reflects all too often both the interests of power and wealth of that "class of statesmen" for whom Machiavelli is one of the first and most brutally dishonest champions, and the demands of an emergent citizenry for whom self-identity has been detached from the sanity of a measured private prudence for the immolatory glories of "My Country, Right or Wrong."[22]

Looking at the more concrete moral consequences from security privatization, a Washington human-rights activist weighing moral implications of the use of mercenaries comments that "watching a Rwanda genocide or a Srebrenica unfold without anyone's lifting a finger is what I find obscene—not using paid professionals to put a stop to it."[23] More specifically, many analysts claim that "had they been allowed, mercenaries would have saved most of the 800,000 innocent people who died during the 1994 genocide in Rwanda—a task that the United States understandably but tragically declined."[24] Similarly, some argue, "if mercenaries had been protecting the Balkan safe havens, there might never have been the massacre of Srebrenica."[25]

The Legitimacy Question

Even the issue of legitimacy itself is contentious. It is clear that "no effective international norms" exist across the board regarding private security forces,[26] and that as a result "little possibility" exists for the emergence of international regimes governing behavior in this area.[27] The same seems true for national norms and the prospects for harmonizing domestic security substitution across states. While it is obviously important to distinguish between legitimate and illegitimate activities of private security providers, some argue "that accepting their presence and in turn discussing regulation could give unfounded legitimacy to something that should be abolished"; whereas others contend "that if they could provide a useful role, then engagement and regulation would be the most appropriate approach."[28] This disagreement is enough all by itself to bring regulatory progress to a standstill.

The spread of privatized security brings into question traditional understandings of the concepts of sovereignty and self-determination of peoples, and these understandings desperately need fresh discussion given the new realities about the possessors of coercive force. How, for example, does the widespread use of private security forces by a national government affect its legitimacy? The international community does not seem even close to being able to answer this question in a satisfactory manner.

It is possible to argue rather pessimistically that the earnest quest for legitimacy by modern private security providers has been a complete failure:

> The careful efforts of private military companies to overcome the negative view of mercenaries were ultimately unsuccessful. The corporatized nature of these firms and their claims to be legitimate and constructive contributors to the international community counted for nothing in the

final analysis: when things went wrong, firms like EO, GSG and Sandline were simply dismissed as "mercenaries," with no government (other than those which had contracted their services in the first place) prepared to accord them legitimacy. Indeed, there has been an increasing movement against the use of transnational security corporations. Some governments have made it difficult for transnational security corporations to operate on their territory, a major impediment to organizing the logistics for what in essence is a military airlift. International financial institutions have even taken to punishing governments using transnational security corporations.[29]

While this presumption of public-relations failure is not universal and in any case has clearly not spelled doom for private security providers, it does underscore the obstacles these companies face in attempting to gain widespread global acceptance.

Clash of Values and Muddled Policy Choices

More generally, privatized security highlights a clash between some basic deeply held liberal internationalist values, reflecting in many ways contradictions embedded in national and international norms. First, there are tensions between the goals of political security and economic profit,[30] revolving around both (1) whether regime perpetuation or revenue maximization should take precedence and (2) whether coercive force should be a market commodity or a prerogative of the state. Second, friction exists between individual and community interests—between personal freedom and collective order—pitting the right to bear arms and to protect one's own against the broader responsibilities to serve the needs of the society as a whole. Third, the simultaneous emphasis on openness and protection creates major strains on the domestic and international levels, as the free movement of people, goods, and services—including privatized security—increases the vulnerability of those indigenous to a particular area to losing complete control over their identity, regime, and way of life. Finally, the joint pursuit of stability and justice embodied in the liberal internationalist tradition is problematic, as state-sponsored private security providers are almost inescapably destined to pursue the first at the expense of the second. Security privatization tends to bring to the surface many of these largely unreconciled issues before either governments or mass publics are ready to deal with them, leading to consequences more in the direction of discomfort and alarm than reasoned compromise.

Equally important, the privatization of security appears to highlight the incongruity of the state continuing to possess the primary right under international law to exert influence in international relations, while at the same time its capacity to provide safety for its citizenry is eroding. Over time, it may appear senseless to accord loyalty to—and have all significant power applications pass through—the institution of national government that can no longer guarantee even the most basic needs of its people. While some would argue that the state has consciously ceded power to private security providers domestically and internationally by outsourcing defense functions to them, and that it could retract that power from these providers back to itself any time it wishes, it may very well be that such outsourcing has fostered difficult-to-reverse ripple effects far beyond what the state ever initially envisioned.

Because of the inherent contradictions in the liberal internationalist view when applied to security privatization, the nature of policy choice to ameliorate the situation is decidedly muddled. The ability of private security forces to coalesce and dissolve and move from place to place with ease,[31] combined with their tendency to be involved in intrastate conflicts where rulers desperately need their services,[32] makes effective global regulation difficult. Widespread global confusion exists about who has the right to hire private security forces (do transnational criminal organizations or terrorists have this privilege?), what rights these forces have within societies, and whose safety these forces enhance. Indeed, the most common state of affairs is that "many of the users of private security and military companies (governments, multinationals and humanitarian organizations) remain ambivalent about the consequences of their use or uncertain about how they should deal with them."[33]

There is not even agreement about how private security providers ought to relate to governments or multinational corporations. Looking first at links to home-state governments, some argue that coordination can be the first step in helping to create restraint and a greater tendency to operate with established international norms, with instability-creating unscrupulous activities eliminated in the process; others look at the specter of this tight relationship between private security companies and home-state governments with great suspicion, assuming the tight relationship could lead to mutual corruption.[34] It is ironic that when private security providers talk to their clients about their relationship to governments, they simultaneously stress their access to government officials and their independence from them,[35] making the relationship between private security providers and home-state governments "a mixture of publicly voiced indignation and tacitly given support."[36] Turning to links to multinational corporations, some argue that most nonmilitarily oriented multinationals have learned to operate well within the global rules of the game, and thus that close ties between these firms and private security providers would lead the latter to behave as responsible global parties. On the other hand, these nonmilitarily oriented multinational corporations (particularly mining companies) are viewed as models of the worst kind of exploitative behavior motivated not by concerns of social welfare but rather by the almighty dollar.

The muddled policy choice has thus far resulted in disappointing global reactions to the spread of privatized security. By and large, "the international community's response to the burgeoning presence of quasi-mercenary organizations has been ambiguous."[37] National governments, particularly in the West, appear unable to come to grips with reality and directly confront their own squeamishness and hypocrisy about confronting the tough choices for managing the deteriorating security predicament in the Third World:

> So, much as with investment, the choice often comes down to mercenary peacekeeping or no peacekeeping. The trouble is that rich governments . . . refuse to acknowledge this bottom line. They find the idea of mercenaries embarrassing. They are cautious about their relationships with firms such as DynCorp, which supplied the police for Bosnia. And the result of this squeamishness is that lots of people die.
>
> Unwilling to commit troops yet unwilling to pronounce the "m" word, governments have devised a peacekeeping system that is mercenary in all but name. Rich countries pay poor-country soldiers to go to dangerous places, either under the banner of the United Nations or in the name of regional super cops such as West Africa's ECOMOG. And the pay is pretty handsome—enough so that poor countries can use the profits to subsidize domestic defense establishments.
>
> This arrangement might be fine if it worked properly. Sadly, it does not.[38]

In reality, of course, such highly artificial arrangements may cosmetically assuage the conscience of Western policymakers, but they do little to manage the underlying problems in the poor countries suffering seemingly endless violence.

The mass public itself appears confused about how to interpret the trend toward privatized security. This public concern persists in part due to "opaque business practices and questionable methods of payment" involved in some of these firms' transactions.[39] There appears to be a widespread "distaste for the private provision of violence and an association of private security companies with the mercenary activity of the

1960s and 70s."[40] The misinformation present in the minds of these on-lookers, fueled in part by sensational reporting about mercenaries on the part of otherwise responsible media sources, exacerbates this problem. Typically, "the press, in knee-jerk reaction, generally derides these modern-day mercenaries with headlines such as 'Guys with Guns,' 'Executive Incomers,' 'Have Gun, Will Prop Up Regime,' and similar titles."[41] The popular media routinely classify "terrorists, drug smugglers, and wandering groups of fanatical religious extremists" as being within the mercenary community,[42] despite evidence that "most acts of rape and pillage, and most military takeovers, are perpetuated by national forces supposedly imbued with the determining motives of a pure patriotism," not by mercenaries.[43] As written in the infamous magazine *Soldier of Fortune*, "too many contemporary policy makers use the word 'mercenary' as if it were the equivalent of syphilis."[44] For whatever reason, it appears to be next to impossible to get balanced coverage of private military forces in the mass media in any country.

This government and mass public confusion is compounded by diffusion of nation-state responsibility for the activities of private security providers. It is evident that "state responsibility for the actions of security companies flows in two directions—responsibility toward the home state which tolerates and 'exports' these companies' services, and responsibility toward the contracting state which enlists and directs the activities of the security company; states on both sides of the contract may attempt to disavow any connection to particular security companies, claiming that the security companies' activities are private."[45] Finger-pointing in all directions results when criticism for ongoing activity takes place.

Conclusion

It is hopefully apparent from discussion in preceding chapters that the privatization of security is sufficiently widespread and influential to warrant careful consideration from the international community. It seems equally clear from this chapter's discussion that a large number of crucial and seemingly insuperable roadblocks stand in the way of such a coherent response. These include the difficulties in defining private security activity and differentiating acceptable from unacceptable motivations; the very mixed track record of security privatization in achieving desired results; the inability to determine optimum conditions for public or private security in terms of its contribution to ending conflict and restoring stability;

Figure 7.1   Roadblocks to Addressing Security Privatization

Inability to Nail Down the Problem
* *Ambiguous Definition and Success of Privatized Security*
  Difficult Delineation of Privatized Security and Distinctive
     Motives
  Mixed Track Record of Effectiveness
  Inability to Determine Optimum Conditions for Public or
     Private Security

Absence of Societal Consensus
* *Contradictory Values and Desires About Privatized Security*
  Conflicting Regulatory Aims of Concerned Groups
  Divisive Questions of Morality and Legitimacy
  Clash Among Deeply Held Liberal Internationalist Values

Lack of Clarity About What to Do
* *Cloudy Policy Choices to Address Privatized Security*
  Government and Citizenry Confusion
  Diffusion of Responsibility
  Ambivalence about Dealing with Privatized Security Issues

the conflicting external regulatory desires of concerned groups regarding private security providers; the underlying question of private security providers' morality or legitimacy; the clash among deeply held liberal internationalist values; the muddled policy choices and government and citizenry confusion surrounding the issue; and the diffusion of responsibility for security privatization. Figure 7.1 summarizes this multitude of roadblocks impeding sound management and oversight of privatized security.

Together these obstacles have stymied policymaking, frustrating both supporters and opponents of security privatization. Consensus building about the privatization of security seems exceedingly more difficult than in other security areas, with sharply differing conceptions about the nature of the problem and little common inspiration about what to do if one could identify the problem.

Notes

1. Jakkie Cilliers and Richard Cornwell, "From the Privatisation of Security to the Privatisation of War?" in Jakkie Cilliers and Peggy Mason, eds., *Peace, Profit or Plunder? The Privatisation of Security in War-Torn African Societies* (Johannesburg: Institute for Security Studies, 1999): p. 241.

2. "Military Companies," *Economist* (January 16, 1999).

3. Robert Mandel, "What Are We Protecting?" *Armed Forces & Society* 22 (spring 1996): 335–355.

4. Ibid.

5. Robert Mandel, *The Changing Face of National Security* (Westport, CT: Greenwood Press, 1994): pp. 12–14.

6. Eboe Hutchful, "Understanding the African Security Crisis," in Abdel-Fatau Musah and J. 'Kayode Fayemi, eds., *Mercenaries: An African Security Dilemma* (London: Pluto Press, 2000): p. 222.

7. Jakkie Cilliers and Christian Dietrich, "Editorial Comment: Privatising Peace Enforcement," *African Security Review* 5 (1996).

8. Francois Misser and Anver Versi, "Soldier of Fortune—The Mercenary as Corporate Executive," *African Business* (December 1997): http://dspace.dial.pipex.com/icpubs/ab/dec97/abcs1201.htm.

9. Deborah D. Avant, "Privatizing Military Training," *Foreign Policy—In Focus* 5 (June 2000): http://www.foreignpolicy-infocus.org/briefs/vol5/v5n17mil.html.

10. International Alert, *The Privatization of Security: Framing a Conflict Prevention and Peacebuilding Policy Agenda* (London: International Alert, April 2001): p. 15.

11. Linda Lebrun, "Mercenary Connections: DiamondWorks, Executive Outcomes, and the New Corporate Military Market," *Attache* (winter 1998–1999): http://www.trinity.utoronto.ca/attache/issues/0001/back_sec.htm.

12. Cilliers and Dietrich, "Editorial Comment."

13. Global Coalition for Africa, "A Consultation on 'The Privatization of Security in Africa'" (Washington, DC: Overseas Development Council, unpublished paper, March 12, 1999).

14. Al J. Venter, "Privatising War" (unpublished paper, May 2000): p. 7.

15. Misser and Versi, "Soldier of Fortune."

16. Global Coalition for Africa, "A Consultation on 'The Privatization of Security in Africa.'"

17. Alex Vines, "Mercenaries, Human Rights and Legality," in Abdel-Fatau Musah and J. 'Kayode Fayemi, eds., *Mercenaries: An African Security Dilemma* (London: Pluto Press, 2000): p.188.

18. Issa A. Mansaray, "Mercenaries: Messiahs of Terror," *Expo Times* (Freetown) (June 8, 2001).

19. Tony Lynch and A. J. Walsh, "The Good Mercenary," *Journal of Political Philosophy* 8 (2000): 133.

20. Ibid., p. 150.

21. Ibid., p. 148.

22. Ibid., p. 134.

23. Sebastian Mallaby, "Mercenaries Are No Altruists, but They Can Do Good," *Washington Post* (June 4, 2001): p. A19.

24. Doug Brooks, "Dogs of Peace," March 7, 1999: http://www.post-gazette. com/forum/19990307edbrooks5.asp.

25. Mallaby, "Mercenaries Are No Altruists," p. A19.

26. Herbert Howe, "Global Order and Security Privatization," *Strategic Forum* 140 (May 1998).

27. James Larry Taulbee, "Mercenaries, Private Armies and Security Companies in Contemporary Policy," *International Politics* 37 (December 2000): 449.

28. International Alert, "Report from 'A Consultation on Private Military Companies'" (London: unpublished paper, December 8, 1998).

29. Kim Richard Nossal, "Bulls to Bears: The Privatization of War in the 1990s": http://www.onwar.org/warandmoney/pdfs/nossal.pdf.

30. Robert Mandel, *Deadly Transfers and the Global Playground* (Westport, CT: Praeger Publishers: 1999): p. 91; Summary of Proceedings, Defense Intelligence Agency Conference, "The Privatization of Security in Sub-Saharan Africa" (Washington, DC: unpublished document, July 24, 1998): pp. 1–2; Janice E. Thomson, *Mercenaries, Pirates, and Sovereigns: State-Building and Extraterritorial Violence in Early Modern Europe* (Princeton, NJ: Princeton University Press, 1994): p. 2.

31. Jeff Herbst, "The Regulation of Private Security Forces," in Greg Mills and John Stremlau, eds., *The Privatisation of Security in Africa* (Johannesburg: South African Institute of International Affairs, 1999): pp. 117–122.

32. Thomas K. Adams, "The New Mercenaries and the Privatization of Conflict," *Parameters* 19 (summer 1999): 103–116.

33. International Alert, *The Privatization of Security*, p. 12.

34. Abdel-Fatau Musah and J. 'Kayode Fayemi, "Africa in Search of Security," in Abdel-Fatau Musah and J. 'Kayode Fayemi, eds., *Mercenaries: An African Security Dilemma* (London: Pluto Press, 2000): p. 18.

35. Ibid.

36. Captain C. J. van Bergen Thirion, "The Privatisation of Security: A Blessing or a Menace?" 1998: http://www.mil.za/CSANDF/CJSupp/TrainingFormation/ DefenceCollege/Researchpapers1998/privatisation_of_security.htm.

37. Lebrun, "Mercenary Connections."

38. Mallaby, "Mercenaries Are No Altruists," p. A19.

39. Global Coalition for Africa, "A Consultation on 'The Privatization of Security in Africa.'"

40. Ibid.

41. Jurgen Brauer, "An Economic Perspective on Mercenaries, Military Companies, and the Privatization of Force," *Cambridge Review of International Affairs* 13 (autumn–winter 1999): 130–146.

42. James R. Davies, *Fortune's Warriors, Private Armies, and the New World Order* (Vancouver, BC: Douglas & McIntire, 2000): chap. 3.

43. Lynch and Walsh, "The Good Mercenary," p. 145.

44. Robert K. Brown, "When Mercenaries Work," *Soldier of Fortune* (May 1999): http://www.sofmag.com/1999sof/0599/cg.html.

45. Juan Carlos Zarate, "The Emergence of a New Dog of War: Private International Security Companies, International Law, and the New World Disorder," *Stanford Journal of International Law* 34 (winter 1998): 92.

8

POSSIBLE POLICY ALTERNATIVES

While the primary purpose of this book is not to provide advice to policymakers, it seems appropriate to consider ways to improve management of privatized security to better serve the desires of nation-states, the rights of the private security providers themselves, and the needs of humanity as a whole. Because such privatization has both costs and benefits, the goal of this quest should be neither to constrain dramatically the operations of private security forces nor to free such groups up to become active in a wider range of predicaments. Rather, the most useful approach from a policy perspective appears to be to attempt to fine-tune the modern use of this age-old coercive instrument. While numerous suggestions for such management of privatized security have emerged from many quarters, many of these ideas appear rather disjointed and ad hoc, not taking into account the full range of options available, the inescapable trade-offs among certain approaches, or the problems surrounding their application. After considering alternatives to the use of privatized security, I use this chapter to discuss general management considerations, the centrality of accountability, and initiatives that might be undertaken at the international-system, nation-state, and community levels.

The Viability of Privatized Security

The conceptual cornerstone for formulating policy alternatives dealing with privatized security is the realization that the evidence does not show convincingly that public security is better than private security. Weighing the dangers and opportunities resulting from the privatization of security mentioned in Chapter 4's general discussion of projected consequences and in Chapter 6's specific summary of case examples, the results here are decidedly mixed. There is no systematically deduced logic or systematically gathered evidence sufficient to defend convincingly why governments are intrinsically better than private security outfits for managing all kinds of security threats. This deficiency is of course parallel to the futility of attempting to demonstrate in a sweeping way why governments are intrinsically better for managing other aspects of society than are other types of private firms. This absence of demonstrated superiority of public over private security applies to the management both of internal threat at home and external threat in other countries.

Without doubt there are those who still contend that, for security threats within countries, "in an ideal world the state would provide for public safety."[1] But to those who make the argument that the application of state power is superior to coercion by private security providers, it is all too easy to point out that these companies "cannot be morally worse than the armies of untrained conscripts and children" so characteristic of government forces in much of the world's recent internal conflicts.[2] Even in debates after the September 11, 2001, terrorist attack on the United States, the widespread claim that placing airport security under federal government rather than private security control would improve passenger safety is fundamentally groundless. Because the application of security privatization today has not differentiated well between those circumstances where it is effective and those where it is ineffective, any set of curative prescriptions needs to try to move the occurrence of privatized security toward those conditions where it operates optimally in the minds of both the involved parties and the international community as a whole.

Similarly, there are voices out there arguing that "in an ideal world . . . strong countries would help war-torn ones by sending in their soldiers."[3] This controversial claim that government-sponsored military assistance is optimal for maintaining stability abroad is in many ways even more difficult to prove convincingly, as the seemingly unending sequence of unsuccessful post–Cold War great power foreign military interventions attests. The sad reality is that nobody has discovered the best way to quell the kinds of turmoil and violence we are witnessing in the current security era, and for that reason one cannot automatically conclude that the use of private security forces is a second-best solution.

Scarce Alternatives to Privatized Security

Throughout this book, an underlying theme has been that, given the current global security predicament, few if any feasible and effective alternatives exist to increased reliance on private security providers. Whether dealing with the needs of domestic police substitution or foreign military assistance, many security policymakers have concluded that their array of possibilities has narrowed dramatically, and indeed in many cases that there are no other avenues to maintain peace and stability. This fatalistic conclusion has usually been a result of the abysmal failure of traditional governmental techniques to maintain order.

In reality, however, at least a few analysts believe strongly that alternative policy options are available in precisely those cases where there has been increased reliance on private security providers to maintain or restore order, exemplified by the set that follows:

> 1. Countries can formally invite other governments to provide advice in reconstituting and training their armed forces.
> 2. In situations of crisis and imminent crisis, the role of private security companies could be played by a United Nations Rapid Reaction Force. It is uncertain whether such a force will be established, but the planning is in an advanced stage.
> 3. If private companies like Executive Outcomes were incorporated into the structures of . . . the UN Office for Peacekeeping, and operated formally under their auspices, the objections raised . . . would fall away.
> 4. The . . . [relevant regional organizations] and the United Nations have to summon the will to take preventive action, which is not reliant on the use of force, before situations of conflict degenerate into crises. The current failure of will of these bodies, their tendency to wait too long before acting, contributes to situations in which desperate governments believe they have no option but to call in mercenaries.[4]

While this line of argument appears to embody considerable idealism in the short run, it demonstrates nonetheless the importance of evaluating carefully other options before turning to security privatization. The basic premise of this chapter's discussion of managing privatized security is that, prior to consideration of any of the regulatory proposals presented, such alternatives have been explored and rejected.

General Management Considerations

The management of private security providers today involves three different functionally visible kinds of restraint.[5] First, restraints emanate from the home states from which these companies emerge, where domestic regulations on arms exports and informal ties to government military and intelligence services may play a key role. Second, restraints emanate from the host states in which these transnational firms operate, where local regulations or temporary integration into government military forces may be in operation. Third, restraints emanate from the global market, where undertaking rash actions such as operating in rogue states, extending conflict for financial gain, working for opposing sides, or committing egregious human-rights violations may seriously jeopardize future business for any private security firm.

Nonetheless, existing national and global restraints using standard operating procedures have largely been insufficient to manage effectively the reemergence of privatized security in the global arena. The combination of home- and host-state national interests with the market forces of supply and demand cannot overcome the limitation that the economic "invisible hand"—maximizing the greater good through individual utility maximization—clearly does not always function properly in security matters.[6] To respond to the ineffectiveness of current restraints by banning completely private security providers is not an option anyone would seriously suggest, and instead constructive engagement appears to be in order.[7] Indeed, attempts to criminalize private security companies would be extremely difficult to enforce in practice,[8] and further might have the backfire effect of driving private military services into a black market[9] where monitoring is next to impossible.

Thus governments, transnational bodies, and international organizations need to discover new means that are both effective and fair to manage the activities of private security providers. The urgency of this need is perhaps best demonstrated by the 1998 "arms to Africa" affair, in which British private security provider Sandline International purportedly signed a contract with the then exiled president of Sierra Leone to supply a major shipment of arms in direct violation of a United Nations embargo.[10] Even if one concluded that little danger is posed today by privatized security, or that security privatization is by and large beneficial, it would appear that a thoughtful assessment of possible policy options designed to maintain existing trends would be appropriate.

Some private security providers argue that they "self-regulate" because their standards conform to those of great-power armies that are their primary source of manpower; they have a clear code of ethics and discipline about who they can and cannot work for, when their services are no longer required, and how their personnel behave in the field; they coordinate their behavior with home government defense establishments; and, most importantly, that if this code is breached, they become

(1) fully exposed to punishment under national and international law and (2) fully vulnerable to dramatic reductions in their future client base and consequently to dissolution as a company.[11] However, these same companies readily admit that they would gain acceptance and legitimacy from some sort of external monitoring of their technical competence, adherence to the law of armed conflict, and respect for human rights.[12]

Of course, if one perceives privatized security as a major threat, the need to reexamine policy responses becomes even more pressing. Pro-regulation skeptics contend that in the future "the geopolitical market may change so that the only available contracts for security companies are with disreputable governments involved in controversial conflicts or with insurgencies."[13] More extreme critics even see private security providers operating internationally simply "as arms purchasing agents for third world countries."[14] Some advocating the need for regulation even point out crucial potential parallels between transnational criminal organizations and private military companies.[15]

The impact of these differences in perspective on the need for new restraints on private security providers is vividly illustrated by the problems[16] surrounding the United Nations General Assembly's 1989 International Convention Against the Recruitment, Use, Financing, and Training of Mercenaries. It requires twenty-two ratifications to come into force, yet only sixteen states have signed up so far. Most Western countries are skeptical that it is enforceable,[17] as being classified as a mercenary necessitates satisfying all six criteria found in the convention, and it is difficult to prove that such is the case. Moreover, some of the signatory states—such as Angola—actually utilize private military companies because they feel these firms do not fall within the legal scope of the convention.

Regardless of one's perspective, however, we do not have as much wisdom as we might expect to rely on from the past. Because mercenaries were considered so much an accepted part of international relations for centuries, there is not a long-standing history of concerted regulatory efforts to draw on as a basis for current policy. Indeed, it is fascinating that until the late 1960s there existed little motivation internationally for limiting mercenary activities.[18] For this reason, any regulatory efforts at the present time would be inescapably quite preliminary.

In any case, avoiding a bureaucratic nightmare with huge costs of implemented policies is crucial to sound management of privatized security. Often high-minded calls for global monitoring, supervision, or regulation end up translating into the unconstrained growth of bureaucracy for its own sake. The depressing reality is that no international regime regulating private security providers could occur without mounds of paperwork, several years of international consultations, annual conferences in The Hague, dozens of contractor studies, several cycles of international legal reviews that may prove controversial and inconclusive, fights inside and between governments on funding and control, and major debates over its charter, terms of reference, scope of authority, location, staffing, coordination, and relationship to the United Nations.

Appropriate Accountability

Looking over the full range of goals surrounding such a private security management effort, none appears to be more important than promoting accountability. Central to the concern about the potential negative impact of private security providers on peace, stability, and human rights "is the lack of accountability and absence of any binding legislation to regulate them."[19] Most analysts agree that an assessment of any security system—public or private—depends on judging both "its efficiency in maintaining some kind of order on the one hand, and its accountability to those people whose security is at stake on the other."[20] With respect to private security providers in particular, the intense international community concern, parallel to worries about pirates in the past and terrorists in the present, "stems from the inherent violence of their profession combined with a lack of control over and accountability for their actions," and a clear way of "distinguishing acceptable and unacceptable types of military services" appears to be through the establishment of accountability to the state.[21]

A widespread but largely erroneous underlying assumption is that private security providers are "obviously less accountable" than public providers.[22] For example, The UN's Special Rapporteur on the Use of Mercenaries contends that "groups of professionals selling their skill in war and violence" are just plain "unaccountable."[23] This premise is ironic given that clients who utilize private outfits often consider them to be far more accountable than governments in the provision of security. Nonetheless, this conclusion in part reflects the legacy of past rogue mercenary activity, and at the same time helps to explain the emphasis of the current crop of private security companies on public relations:

> The new mercenaries have perfected their public relations and legal jargon so as to divert prying eyes and confuse the trail of the web of intrigues and deals surrounding the supposedly altruistic notions of

saving "legitimate" governments from "warlords" and "barbaric thugs." These amateurishly disguised tracks of their corporate web also help explain the inextricable linkage of mercenaries to the issues of instability, light weapons proliferation and protracted conflict in their regions of operation.[24]

Advocates of this cynical premise argue for imposing the most elaborate and explicit forms of accountability on private military providers as virtually the only way to expose and eradicate the successful sham that these companies have perpetrated on the international community.

It might indeed be possible to impose such accountability on even the most rogue groups of mercenaries:

> The critics charge that mercenaries won't be held accountable for battlefield atrocities. But Nigerian troops committed plenty of unpunished atrocities in the course of Sierra Leone peacekeeping. If the United Nations hired a private firm of mercenaries for peacekeeping, it could write accountability into the contract—and enforce that contract much more readily than it can discipline a wayward government.[25]

According to this logic, combination of governments, international organizations, multinational corporations, and humanitarian agencies could be involved to ensure the private security providers of all stripes stay on the right track.[26] If there is one thing private security providers appear to understand and abide by, more than government troops asked to engage in unusual overseas operations conducted under international auspices, it is the codified conditions specified for their hire in the contracts they sign as preconditions for receiving payment.

However, before heading down the road of creating elaborate accountability regimes, there needs to be systematic establishment of the actual need—in terms of identifying the exact problem being solved, actions being monitored, and appropriate groups to which private security providers are held accountable—in a way that has not been done so far with regard to privatized security. This last issue proves to be particularly thorny: while state governments employ most private military companies, many private security providers work for nonstate groups; in such cases, should these companies be accountable to the government or the nonstate employers (goals and expectations might differ)? Moreover, perhaps it is ultimately the people within societies—not the government defense establishment—to whom private security providers ought to be accountable, as some governments may downplay or ignore the interests of their people. Indeed, there are those who feel that the more critical accountability from a democratic perspective is to the civilian elements within the state.[27] In cases where government regimes are in transition or are experiencing a crisis of legitimacy, this question becomes particularly salient.

It is also important to determine at the outset what kinds of wrongdoing by these outfits would be considered out of bounds, which existing formal and informal regulatory structures exist to address these areas of concern, and why these structures are inadequate. The prerequisites for moving toward new forms of accountability thus include demonstration that (1) a serious problem in accountability exists; (2) no other existing mechanism can solve that problem, as other alternatives have been exhausted; (3) implementation of a new accountability regime is feasible politically, economically, legally, and operationally; (4) a new accountability regime is likely to be effective; and (5) such a regime would be worth the trouble and expense involved.

One of the underlying problems here is that the desire to impose new accountability standards on private security providers may be based not so much on evidence of violation of national and international laws by the current crop of companies but rather more heavily on a combination of lawless activities by mercenaries in earlier eras and apprehensions about what might happen in the future. This kind of motivation, focusing on hypothetical or historical violations, faces inherent limitations and ambiguities. Justifying regulatory movement among reluctant parties is particularly difficult under such conditions.

In any case, just as private security providers intend to augment rather than replace state-sponsored security, whatever accountability system emerges needs to support rather than supplant existing national and international laws and law enforcement mechanisms. Moreover, such a system should take fully into account the already functioning safeguards provided by the intense scrutiny from nongovernmental organizations, such as Human Rights Watch and Amnesty International, that are highly vocal and vigilant and well connected to the U.S. Congress and its counterparts in other nations. These influential transnational groups have had a more than decent track record in bringing to the attention of the international community any infractions by private security providers.

International System Initiatives

Transparency is by far the most popular suggestion among both private military companies and their critics.[28] The greater information disclosure resulting from this transparency, presumably monitored by an international body, could allow governments, international organizations, and transnational watchdog groups to become better informed about the scope and nature of private security activity, thus improving understanding of what areas of irregular behavior need special attention. This approach could directly address widespread concerns about the ability of these private firms to conceal their list of clients and activities from the public eye. However, within the "characteristically murky area of covert operations" in which private security providers frequently operate, even today "access to information still essentially depends on investigative journalism."[29] A much more formal system of information exchange, with regular monitoring in place, may be necessary to help both prevent abuses and to alleviate the widespread suspicions about unsavory activities taking place under the guise of privatized security.

A potentially more dramatic idea is global regulation that requires private security providers to secure approval of their particular projects and possibly even to submit themselves to full operational oversight by an international body. Paid for by the international community, but formulated and agreed upon mutually by governments, international organizations, and the private security providers themselves, this system could prevent private security providers from engaging in egregious violations of established norms and from playing one country off against another in terms of different standards of behavior. For example, some recommend that private security providers ought not to work for governments that are not universally recognized, and ought not to undertake acts that might lead to internal repression or looting and plunder.[30] Others even suggest the establishment of a UN-sponsored international security industry commission to help with this kind of global regulation of private security companies.[31] Strengthening international conventions covering mercenaries could in many onlookers' minds be a helpful first step in this general direction.[32]

Imposing a code of conduct, again through an international body, is a related common system-level proposal. Such a code could roughly standardize across national boundaries the restrictions on behavior applying to private military activity, for both domestic substitution and foreign assistance, so that it would not be left to the nations in which this activity operates to have to formulate and enforce necessary procedures. Several transnational organizations, including multinational corporations and humanitarian agencies, have already developed and imposed such codes of conduct on private security companies they hire,[33] and several private security providers have already formulated and implemented their own self-imposed code of conduct. Some examples of how such a code would work include guidelines about the types of clients private security providers could work for, the kinds of tactics private armies could employ in the battlefield, the variety of restrictions related to human-rights issues, the sort of payment private security providers could demand, and the nature of the relationship such providers should have with the home government (of the country from which the company originates) and the host government (of the country in which the company provides private security services).

Aside from these oft-mentioned general suggestions, there are some more particular calls to address more specialized international system concerns about the connections between private security providers and presumably unsavory domestic and foreign groups.[34] For example, some want to restrain the controversial link between private military companies and international mining corporations: the worry is that while private security companies often say that their goal is to restore democratically elected governments to power, or to keep such regimes in power, the reality is that the protection (or even acquisition) of precious minerals may play a major role. Others want to restrict a certain set of undesirable covert ties between private security providers and home-state governments, as the secret use of these firms to carry out foreign policy, often called "covert proxyization," is considered detrimental to regime accountability. Still others want to narrow the tricky connection between private security vendors and arms-brokering agents, in which these companies bear some responsibility for accelerating the entrance of sizable numbers of light weapons into a war-torn region, and suggest the possibility that existing arms-export control regimes expand to cover private security company activities that may evade traditional arms-export licensing procedures.

However, these more specialized global sanctions are extremely difficult to formulate and implement fairly. Circumstances differ across regions, and what constitutes an undesirable connection in one area may be a crucial legitimate link in another. Resource extraction, home-state corporation ties, and arms transfer represent complex challenges for state-to-state regulation all by themselves, and to attempt to devise regulatory policy to restrict the activity of private security providers on these issues would appear to pose nearly insuperable obstacles. Most generally, attempting to devise universal (in time and space) policies to restrict the ways in which private security outfits interact with other legitimate domestically and internationally sanctioned organizations appears to be unwise.

Indeed, when looking at the full range of management schemes initiated at the international system level, considering not only fairness but feasibility, their probable utility looks dismal. Control of private security companies by international organizations, requiring the cooperation of state governments, has inherent weaknesses vividly highlighted by the inability of the United Nations to get more signatories to the General Assembly's 1989 International Convention Against the Recruitment, Use, Financing, and Training of Mercenaries. The possibilities for coordinated and effective international organization response to privatized security thus appear to be quite low.

Nation-State Initiatives

Given the general infeasibility of an international regulatory regime at the present time, two options clearly remain—relying on either home- or host-state government initiatives. Unfortunately, the almost inevitable structural and functional weaknesses found within those host-state governments choosing to rely on foreign private military help makes these regimes a decidedly imprudent choice for imposing new or more coherent restraints on private security providers. Instead, it would appear that the greatest chance for meaningful regulation in the near future would center primarily on home-state governments.

Many analysts adamantly argue that "it is the primary responsibility of governments in supplier countries to regulate the activities of private military companies operating globally from within their territory."[35] Looking at current trends realistically, "long term survival for any private military company depends upon home government sponsorship," and thus the possibility exists that "domestic regulation can play a role in separating the marginal organizations whose credo is 'have guns, will travel for money' from companies with a more responsible ethic."[36] In facing the possibility that private security companies can easily relocate their headquarters to more conducive locations if too stringent legislation is applied in a particular country,[37] movement toward harmonization of national home-state procedures could help set common standards, eventually forming the basis for multilateral coordination regarding the use and operation of private security companies.[38] Although complete harmonization is somewhat of a pipe dream, even if partial harmonization developed, then private service providers would face a much more restricted range of cross-national movement choices.

There is, however, a clear danger involved in relying on home states to manage domestic and international private security providers. It is evident that "when governments exert control over security companies' profitability or ability to operate efficiently, security companies will become attuned to the needs of the state and will align their operations with the state's interests."[39] The occasions when these firms are directly involved in combat are of particular concern. There is a tricky balance to achieve here between making sure that a private security provider is genuinely responsible to its home state and at the same time making sure that the home-state government is not able to respond to this relationship irresponsibly by using the private security provider in ways that would be unacceptable to the domestic public or the international community. If such onlookers are ever going to accept privatized security activity, then the home government must demonstrate that it applies strictly a carefully constructed set of sound—consistent, fair, and ultimately predictable—principles for selecting what gets approved and evaluating how approved activities turn out. These principles need to be relatively immune to the whims of immediate political expediency, involving an examination before and after approval of the implications of privatized activity for both national interests and international stability.

While appropriate home-state-oriented legislation—if properly formulated and implemented—has the potential to help out quite a bit, some significant implementation questions remain. Two key uncertainties are: "(1) whether a 'core' group of Western states can agree among themselves on a common and effective set of regulatory criteria and (2) whether these states can exercise sufficient leverage over potential delinquents to make a real difference on the ground."[40] A related concern emerges about what to do if the performance of an outsourced privatized security activity is unsatisfactory: if a home government declares that a delivered service is inadequate, it may have to take the time, trouble, and energy to demonstrate this to teams of government and corporation lawyers, exercising clauses in contracts that may be disputed and open to interpretation, instead of just being able to take direct management action over in-house government resources. Furthermore, if a private security company's home government develops interests that clash with the company's host-state employer, it is unclear who does or should call the shots; the widespread tentative leaning thus far—for better or for worse—appears to be that such companies operate in the strategic interests of their home states.[41]

Keeping in mind the bureaucratic-nightmare specter raised earlier, there need to be more carefully scrutinized yet more streamlined ways for new policies to work their way through the Byzantine channels of home-state governments. In the United States today, for example, the government monitors such U.S. firms operating abroad through the 1968 Arms Export Control Act, requiring that each company exporting arms or military-related services register with the U.S. government and receive a license for each contract. Since March 1998, the implementation of this act is under the International Traffic in Arms Regulations, overseen by the Office of Defense Trade Controls in the Bureau of Political-Military Affairs in the State Department (with enforcement undertaken largely by the Customs Service). The problem is that the State Department "handles their export licensing in much the same way as it would a crate of guns,"[42] lacking the kind of carefully specified criteria and close scrutiny necessary for this process to become meaningful. So even though the State Department has rejected private military company proposals on more than one occasion, effective lobbying and appeal to the "if-we-don't-go-in-someone-else-will" principle seems to have made it somewhat of a toothless watchdog. While the U.S. Department of Defense also plays a major role in arms-export controls, it cannot by itself effectively regulate what is done with arms and with paramilitary forces for hire.

There are, however, built-in incentives for home-state governments to take a much more concerted effort at managing privatized security. While "the United States, the United Kingdom and France have no interest in driving companies offshore or in an international regime which would remove certification and approval of missions from national authorities,"[43] these countries do have a direct national interest in keeping their international active private security providers sufficiently in check so as to avoid international embarrassment or humiliation. In any case, private security companies "have strong personal and professional links to the governments and militaries of their respective home states,"[44] reinforcing the potential for mutually beneficial cooperation here through home-state use of informal means of influence.

More specifically, a popular proposal is tighter licensing and certification or registration procedures of private security providers,[45] both of which make the most sense when initiated by home states (though at a later point international coordination could emerge). Observers who are most enthusiastic about assigning responsibility to exporting states as the means of effectively regulating private security providers tend to promote national registration and contract-specific licensing regimes.[46] Licensing or certification for those private providers of security could guarantee qualifications, training, and experience in such a way that the purchaser of these services—whether government, international organization, or individual—might be able to count on a certain level of effectiveness. The basis for approving licensing applications for private security providers could include such criteria as whether their activities would violate international embargoes, contribute to external aggression, undermine economic development, and jeopardize public security.[47] The licensing and registration procedures could, assuming monitoring and enforcement costs are managed effectively, work in regulating both private domestic security substitution and foreign security assistance.

Others propose restraining private security providers by increased arms-transfer restrictions across nations and increased gun control within nations to prevent weapons from getting into the hands of private groups,[48] with home states restricting arms exports at the same time they crack down on weapons within their borders. These onlookers believe that the problems with privatized security stem from their association with the availability of instruments of violence. However, even though this approach links up well with the grass-roots concerns of vocal subnational groups, in many ways it appears to address symptoms rather than root causes of security privatization dangers.

Finally, there are those who recommend limits on the time and scope of private presence. Such limits could involve making sure that no government permanently assigns the vast majority of its security functions to private groups, or that no country would feel saddled with privatized security beyond the time when such an instrument proved to be most necessary for management of ongoing turmoil. There is strong feeling that extraterritorial applications of privatized security, in particular, should be subject to such limits, reflecting the transitional nature of the problems these applications address.[49] The downside of this approach is it restricts the flexibility of privatized security to cope with changing needs that render initial expectations and agreements outmoded, thus eliminating one of the major advantages of private over public coercion; sometimes the assurance of a long-term or expanding presence of private military forces might actually be desirable from a mass public, government, or international-community perspective.

Community Initiatives

Most analysts examining security privatization on the global level suggest that the target of any emerging regulatory policies ought to be at the supply end, focusing on the private security providers themselves.

In their emphasis on these companies, these observers are loathe to hamstring national governments, either the home states from which these private providers emerge or the host states to which these private providers contribute their services; and appear even more reluctant to restrict the right of private individuals, groups, or local communities to use privatized security. This prevalent "hands-off" attitude is due at least in part to these onlookers' feeling that the source of potential abuses lies primarily in the security companies, not in national governments or the individuals hiring them. According to this logic, it seems as if the fault lies not in misguided logic by states or individuals choosing to use private coercion to achieve their ends, but rather in the ways in which private security providers respond to the situations in which they are employed.

However, this book's explanatory analysis suggests a much more fundamental—and far less discussed—approach to address the growing spread of security privatization. In addition to considering as a target the providers or tools of this protection, it suggests taking a very close look at the demand side of the equation—addressing the plight of the recipients and the reasons they feel they need privatized security so desperately. Although it is not the nation-states purchasing private military services "who attract the moral barbs of social commentators," perhaps it should be, as such use may be "a sign of the corruption of the body politic" or of regimes that "no longer command the respect or allegiance of their citizens"; indeed, it is possible that "in a world in which national armies and the attendant patriotic fervour are ubiquitous, the need for mercenaries becomes a litmus test of the illegitimacy of those rulers who require them."[50] What are the dangers clients fear, and is there any way (outside of privatized security) to reduce these threats? What are the reasons behind the inability of state governments to manage their own internal security problems, and why are other national governments so reluctant to help out in such situations? Addressing the roots of existing security dangers, with an aim toward minimizing them, seems crucial as an alternative to the simple acceptance of their continued existence, reliance on private security providers for protection, and assignment of blame to these companies when things do not turn out well.

These demand-oriented concerns indicate a certain senselessness in worrying exclusively about private security providers and not for the states and multinational corporations who employ them. In many analysts' view, "it is not the private military companies themselves who should be singled out—they are, like any good economist, attempting to meet the demand with their supply—but rather the countries who hire them or who allow transnational corporations (particularly in the mining and oil exploration fields) to use them."[51] Governments and corporations may accordingly need some limits on their unbridled freedom to use private security providers anywhere and everywhere they see fit. While restraining the behavior of private security providers is a lot more globally acceptable than restraining the behavior of legitimate duly elected national governments and widely respected multinational corporations, both could be essential parts of sound security management.

Among the best vantage points for scrutinizing the demand for security privatization is the community level, rather than the international-system or nation-state levels. Many of the reasons governments are outsourcing functions traditionally associated with state control relate heavily to changes in the demands of citizenry within their borders. Moreover, many of those choosing to employ private security providers are not governments but societal groups fearful about their degree of protection.

To address demand directly, there is a specific need for special kinds of discussion within and across participating states of a type that has not occurred very much in the past. A crucial starting point would be getting people with experience both on the military and civilian contractor side together to engage in serious and frank conversations about how best to use private security providers to assist with government operations—there would need to be open and honest debate about what has worked, what has failed, and what is and is not politically feasible. After such deliberations, involvement of others from legislative and executive branches of government to work on mutually satisfactory regulation would increase the chances of its success. Later on, of course, discussion with the mass public leading to support or at least minimal understanding on its part would be a real asset for long-term effectiveness.

While many obstacles have existed preventing this kind of sustained dialogue, both national home-state governments and transnational private security providers are beginning to recognize that it is in their mutual interest to initiate such open discussion "to help remove some of the confusion that exists and stifles the development of practical policies" pertaining to security privatization.[52] We need to have more discussion and build more agreement about the acceptable types of private coercion, the occasions for its use, and the choice of who implements it. Indeed, the appropriate role of coercion—both public and private—as the accepted means of managing insecurity could use a fresh look. Differing views held among factions of the mass public about the adequacy or inadequacy of existing levels of security and about ways of improving protection need direct confrontation and possible reconciliation. Moreover, this discussion needs to take place within the broader context of what kind of security we want and what our underlying notions are about peace, stability, and justice.

A key implication of addressing demand would be a different role for local communities themselves with regard to security privatization. It seems important that these communities begin to take more responsibility for side effects of private security activity they initiate, or are initiated by others affecting them, particularly with regard to human-rights concerns.[53] Such responsibility would require that if unforeseen repercussions from private security activity developed in surrounding areas, the communities would enter into discussions with private security providers to find some way to address them. In focusing the attention of such communities on scrutinizing these unanticipated consequences, this strategy might even cause some to realize that sound community governance could reduce the need for private security services.[54] This approach could also represent a first step toward establishing some community-based social accountability among private security providers.

For people concerned about negative implications from privatized security, having those who request the use of private security services become an explicit target—in addition to those providing these services—could mean that the decision to move in this direction is made more wisely. Those living in failing states or experiencing domestic violence may indeed, with eyes wide open, choose privatized security involving the application of coercion as the best way to achieve a short-term feeling of safety; but they would become aware (despite the absence of readily available alternatives) of the possible long-term dependence this may engender, the possible futility of isolated pockets of safety within an unsafe interdependent global setting, and the possible inability of this approach to reduce substantially the growth of the dangers outside of their often temporarily protected enclaves. Part of what is needed, of course, is the development of better conflict-prevention mechanisms in areas where turmoil and strife have become an almost permanent part of the political landscape.[55]

Without addressing the reasons why more clients are emerging who want to use private security providers, any efforts to regulate these companies may prove to be futile. In other words, if the perceived need remains untouched, then any national or international regulations on privatized security may end up being circumvented. While clearly there is no desire to eliminate any need to turn to privatized protection, at the

very least some efforts could occur—with considerable potential benefit—to reevaluate the nature of this demand.

Conclusion

While few would argue that the privatization of security is the very best
means of providing safety for the world's citizenry, this book has identified many situations where other protective options are not—and do
not appear likely to be in the foreseeable future—readily available. For
this reason, it is essential that scholars and policymakers alike devote
more attention to identifying and promoting circumstances when private
security providers serve the public as well as the private good. We need
to find ways to move beyond the polemical close-minded arguments on
both sides of the security privatization debate to try to make privatized
security work, within the context of those carefully limited instances
when it is employed.

   The long-term prognosis for the global survival and spread of private security providers appears bright, but not without a few bumps in
the road. Uncomfortable as many people are with some types of security
privatization, this form of protection is going to be with us for quite a
while. In reality, however, many security companies are poorly managed and therefore short-lived or do not possess the combination of
skills and tools necessary to manage the risks and dangers they confront, and many of their clients are unable to investigate effectively the
credentials of these companies; these limitations severely limit the credibility of this emerging industry[56]: survival on the international level involves "a difficult balancing act," particularly for smaller security
providers or those offering direct combat services, given that many
"projects are invariably in war zones or other regions of conflict" where
private security firms compete for a few contracts without full home
government support. However, prevailing security forecasts for the next
couple of decades indicate that the kinds of unstable predicaments calling for security privatization are likely to increase, while the ability and
willingness to manage the turmoil of other parties—particularly nation-
states and international organizations attempting state-sponsored peacekeeping—is likely to decrease.

   This chapter has tentatively outlined some ideas that might help in addressing the privatization in today's world. While it presents and discusses
many possibilities, its strongest and most urgent advocacy emerges for increasing transparency by private security providers, utilizing home-state

governments as the primary source of regulation, and addressing the reasons behind the demand for privatized security in addition to its supply. In terms of actionable recommendations, it is clear that we must simultaneously (1) reduce the demand for the most redundant or inefficient uses of privatized security; (2) increase the use of private security providers in those circumstances where government security forces are less effective; and (3) make sure that any such use has substantial monitoring and accountability. In the process, both governments and private security providers need to come to grips directly and honestly with their own limitations as well as capabilities when it comes to coercion. It is important simultaneously to narrow and focus the applications of private security providers and to keep these applications more in tune with the changing norms of the domestic and international communities. Any action should occur not in a vacuum but rather in light of a deeper understanding of security privatization's relationship to broader security trends discussed in Chapter 2, its complex web of causes and consequences discussed in Chapters 3 and 4, and the obstacles improved management has traditionally faced discussed in Chapter 7. Figure 8.1 summarizes the ways of addressing the privatization of security.

In particular, the unconventional taxonomy of privatized security presented in Chapter 5—revealing key distinctions in scope, source, form, and purpose—demonstrates how important it is not to treat all manifestations of this phenomenon as a unified homogeneous whole, while at the same time not isolating management of each interconnected strand. We may very well need different management techniques for all the different varieties of security privatization, but having a certain coherence among all of the varieties of this phenomenon seems essential for both legitimacy and effectiveness. It is important to assess the mutual compatibility among the many types of privatized security—domestic and international, top-down and bottom-up, combat support and military advice, and status quo and non–status quo. What is most needed is a practical assessment of which forms of private security are most nationally and internationally beneficial or detrimental, considering spillovers and short-run and long-run implications for stability or instability, with the result being the proliferation of the more desirable— and disappearance of the less desirable—manifestations. This book provides an initial road map of how to proceed in that direction.

Without consideration of fresh, creative security thinking to address this growing phenomenon, there is a distinct possibility that efforts to reduce the spiraling anarchic violence within and across societies will actually be thwarted by the spread of privatized security, with protected

Figure 8.1   Managing the Privatization of Security

**International System Initiatives
Concerning Privatized Security**
- *Openness and Standardization*
  Greater transparency involving increased information disclosure,
  with external monitoring of technical competence, adherence to
  the law, and respect for human rights
    Movement toward international code of conduct
    Approval of private security projects and operational over-
  sight by the international community, with policies mutually
  agreed upon by governments, international organizations, and
  private security providers
    Costs of initiatives largely underwritten by the international
  community

Nation-State Initiatives Concerning Privatized Security
- *Governmentally Enforced Restraints*
  Focus on home-state government regulation of private security
  providers
    Registration or certification of private military companies,
  with tighter national licensing procedures
    Increased arms-export restrictions across nations and increased
  gun control within nations
    Limits on the time and scope of contracts, with built-in ex
  post facto cost-benefit analysis

**Community-Level Initiatives Concerning
Privatized Security**
- *Enhanced Mutual Responsibility*
  Addressing the demand side—why people feel they need privatized protection—as well as the supply side—the providers or the
  tools of this protection
    Establishing accountability by private security providers for
  unintended consequences
    Getting experienced military and civilian contractors together
  to engage in frank conversation about how best to use private security providers and about what has worked, what has failed, and
  what is and is not politically feasible
    Discussion and consensus building with the mass public
  about the acceptable types of private coercion, the occasions for
  its use, and the choice of who implements it within the broader
  context of accepted notions of peace, stability, and justice

---

groups—as well as those protecting them—becoming more ostrich-like in their unconcern for what goes on outside the sphere of their privatized safety. No amount of regulation of private security forces or weaponry will begin to induce those experiencing privatized security to think about the welfare of the broader community, whether it be getting MPRI-protected Croats or Bosnians to think about the whole of the former Yugoslavia or getting security guards protecting a gated community in Beverly Hills to think about the whole of Los Angeles. Ultimately, then, a concerted move to bolster and reclarify the social contract between rulers and the ruled about mutual security responsibility appears to be a crucial prerequisite to transforming the privatization of security into a truly constructive force in modern global society.

Notes

1. Sebastian Mallaby, "Mercenaries Are No Altruists, but They Can Do Good," *Washington Post* (June 4, 2001): p. A19.

2. Douglas Brooks, "Write a Cheque, End a War: Using Private Military Companies to End African Conflicts," *Conflict Trends Magazine* (June 2000).

3. Mallaby, "Mercenaries Are No Altruists," p. A19.

4. Laurie Nathan, "'Trust Me I'm a Mercenary': The Lethal Danger of Mercenaries in Africa" (Seminar on the Privatisation of Peacekeeping Institute for Security Studies, February 20, 1997): http://ccrweb.ccr.uct.ac.za/staff_papers/laurie_merc.html.

5. Patrick J. Cullen, "Keeping the New Dog of War on a Tight Leash: Assessing Means of Accountability for Private Military Companies," *Conflict Trends Magazine* (Spring 2000).

6. Robert Mandel, *Deadly Transfers and the Global Playground* (Westport, CT: Praeger Publishers, 1999): p. 111.

7. David Shearer, *Private Armies and Military Intervention* (London: Oxford University Press, International Institute for Strategic Studies Adelphi Paper 316, 1998): pp. 74–77.

8. Global Coalition for Africa, "A Consultation on 'The Privatization of Security in Africa'" (Washington, DC: Overseas Development Council, unpublished paper, March 12, 1999).

9. Juan Carlos Zarate, "The Emergence of a New Dog of War: Private International Security Companies, International Law, and the New World Disorder," *Stanford Journal of International Law* 34 (winter 1998): 152.

10. Chaloka Beyani and Damian Lilly, *Regulating Private Military Companies* (London: International Alert, August 2001): p. 9.

11. Sandline International, "Private Military Companies—Independent or Regulated?" (London: Sandline International, unpublished paper, March 28, 1998): http://www.sandline.com.

12. Ibid.

13. Zarate, "The Emergence of a New Dog of War," p. 80.

14. Issa A. Mansaray, "Mercenaries: Messiahs of Terror," *Expo Times* (Freetown) (June 8, 2001).

15. Mark Duffield, "The New Corporate Armies" (1999): http://cornerhouse. icaap.org/briefings/12.html.

16. Douglas Farah, "Cartel Hires Mercenaries to Train Security Forces," *Washington Post* (November 4, 1997): p. A12.

17. Abdel-Fatau Musah and J. 'Kayode Fayemi, eds., *Mercenaries: An African Security Dilemma* (London: Pluto Press, 2000): p. ix.

18. James R. Davies, *Fortune's Warriors, Private Armies, and the New World Order* (Vancouver, BC: Douglas & McIntire, 2000): chapter 3.

19. Beyani and Lilly, Regulating Private Military Companies, p. 4.

20. Jakkie Cilliers and Richard Cornwell, "From the Privatisation of Security to the Privatisation of War?" in Jakkie Cilliers and Peggy Mason, eds., *Peace, Profit or Plunder? The Privatisation of Security in War-Torn African Societies* (Johannesburg: Institute for Security Studies, 1999): p. 240.

21. Zarate, "The Emergence of a New Dog of War," pp. 77, 119.

22. Musah and Fayemi, *Mercenaries*, p. ix.

23. Linda Lebrun, "Mercenary Connections: DiamondWorks, Executive Outcomes, and the New Corporate Military Market," *Attache* (winter 1998–1999): http://www.trinity.utoronto.ca/attache/issues/0001/back_sec.htm.

24. Abdel-Fatau Musah and J. 'Kayode Fayemi, "Africa in Search of Security: Mercenaries and Conflicts—An Overview," in Abdel-Fatau Musah and J. 'Kayode Fayemi, eds., *Mercenaries: An African Security Dilemma* (London: Pluto Press, 2000): p. 25.

25. Mallaby, "Mercenaries Are No Altruists," p. A19.

26. International Alert, *The Privatization of Security: Framing a Conflict Prevention and Peacebuilding Policy Agenda* (London: International Alert, April 2001): p. 7.

27. Deborah Avant, "The Market for Force: Exploring the Privatization of Military Services" (New York: paper presented at the Council on Foreign Relations, Study Group on Arms Trade and Transnationalization of Defense, 1999).

28. Shearer, *Private Armies and Military Intervention*, p. 77; Interview with Ed Soyster, vice president for operations, MPRI, Alexandria, VA, July 14, 1999; Sandline International, "Should the Activities of Private Military Companies be Transparent?" (London: unpublished paper, September 1998); John Harker, "Mercenaries: Private Power, Public Insecurity?" *Life & Peace Institute* (April 1998): http://www.life-peace.org/nroutes/merc498.htm, p. 8.

29. International Alert, *The Privatization of Security*, p. 9.

30. Beyani and Lilly, *Regulating Private Military Companies*, p. 7.

31. Davies, *Fortune's Warriors, Private Armies*, chap. 9.

32. Owen Greene, "From Mercenaries to Private Security Companies: Options for Future Policy Research," presentation at a Consultation on Private Military Companies held at the International Alert Offices in London on December 8, 1998; International Alert, "An Assessment of the Mercenary Issue at the Fifty-Fifth Session of the UN Commission on Human Rights" (unpublished paper, May 1999); Summary of Proceedings, Defense Intelligence Agency

Conference, "The Privatization of Security in Sub-Saharan Africa" (Washington, DC: unpublished document, July 24, 1998): pp. 1–2.

33. Damian Lilly, *The Privatization of Security and Peacebuilding* (London: International Alert, September 2000): p. 30.

34. International Alert, "Report from 'A Consultation on Private Military Companies'" (London: unpublished paper, December 8, 1998).

35. Beyani and Lilly, *Regulating Private Military Companies*, p. 21.

36. James Larry Taulbee, "Mercenaries, Private Armies and Security Companies in Contemporary Policy," *International Politics* 37 (December 2000): 448–449.

37. Musah and Fayemi, *Mercenaries*, p. ix.

38. Global Coalition for Africa, "A Consultation on 'The Privatization of Security in Africa.'"

39. Zarate, "The Emergence of a New Dog of War," p. 80.

40. International Alert, *The Privatization of Security*, p. 9.

41. Avant, "The Market for Force."

42. Justin Brown, "The Rise of the Private-Sector Military," *Christian Science Monitor* (July 5, 2000): p. 3.

43. Taulbee, "Mercenaries, Private Armies," p. 449.

44. Zarate, "The Emergence of a New Dog of War," p. 76.

45. Greene, "From Mercenaries to Private Security Companies"; International Alert, "An Assessment of the Mercenary Issue"; Summary of Proceedings, "The Privatization of Security," pp. 1–2.

46. Zarate, "The Emergence of a New Dog of War," p. 154.

47. Beyani and Lilly, *Regulating Private Military Companies*, p. 7.

48. Private Communication from Michael Renner, June 3, 1999; International Alert, "Executive Summary of a Consultation on Private Military Companies" (London: unpublished paper, December 8, 1998): p. 1.

49. International Alert, *The Privatization of Security*, p. 56.

50. Tony Lynch and A. J. Walsh, "The Good Mercenary," *Journal of Political Philosophy* 8 (2000): 149.

51. Kevin A. O'Brien, "Private Military Companies and African Security 1990–1998," in Abdel-Fatau Musah and J. 'Kayode Fayemi, eds., *Mercenaries: An African Security Dilemma* (London: Pluto Press, 2000): p. 44.

52. International Alert, *The Privatization of Security*, p. 28.

53. Lilly, *The Privatization of Security and Peacebuilding*, p. 24.

54. International Alert, *The Privatization of Security*, p. 56.

55. Musah and Fayemi, *Mercenaries*, p. x.

56. Davies, *Fortune's Warriors, Private Armies*, chap. 8.

SELECTED BIBLIOGRAPHY

Adams, Thomas K. "The New Mercenaries and the Privatization of Conflict," *Parameters* 19 (summer 1999): 103–116.

Alexander, John B. *Future War* (New York: Thomas Dunne Books, 1999).

Avant, Deborah. "From Mercenaries to Citizen Armies: Explaining Change in the Practice of War," *International Organization* 54 (winter 2000): 41–72.

Blakely, Edward J., and Mary Gail Snyder. *Fortress America: Gated Communities in the United States* (Washington, DC: Brookings Institution, 1997).

Boutwell, Jeffrey, Michael T. Klare, and Laura W. Reed, eds. *Lethal Commerce* (Cambridge, MA: Committee on International Security Studies of the American Academy of Arts and Sciences, 1995).

Brauer, Jurgen. "An Economic Perspective on Mercenaries, Military Companies, and the Privatization of Force," *Cambridge Review of International Affairs* 13 (autumn–winter 1999): 130–146.

Cilliers, Jakkie, and Peggy Mason, eds. *Peace, Profit or Plunder? The Privatisation of Security in War-Torn African Societies* (Johannesburg: Institute for Security Studies, 1999).

Davies, James R. *Fortune's Warriors, Private Armies, and the New World Order* (Vancouver, BC: Douglas & McIntire, 2000).

Feigenbaum, Harvey, Jeffrey Henig, and Chris Hamnett. *Shrinking the State: The Political Underpinnings of Privatization* (Cambridge: Cambridge University Press, 1999).

Howe, Herbert M. *Ambiguous Order: Military Forces in African States* (Boulder: Lynne Rienner, 2001).

International Alert. *The Privatization of Security: Framing a Conflict Prevention and Peacebuilding Policy Agenda* (London: International Alert, April 2001).

Isenberg, David. *Soldiers of Fortune Ltd.: A Profile of Today's Private Sector Corporate Mercenary Firms* (Washington DC: Center for Defense Information Monograph, November 1997).

Lynch, Tony, and A. J. Walsh. "The Good Mercenary," *Journal of Political Philosophy* 8 (2000): 141.

165

Mandel, Robert. *Deadly Transfers and the Global Playground* (Westport, CT: Praeger, 1999).

Mills, Greg, and John Stremlau, eds. *The Privatisation of Security in Africa* (Johannesburg: South African Institute of International Affairs, 1999).

Musah, Abdel-Fatau, and J. 'Kayode Fayemi, eds. *Mercenaries: An African Security Dilemma* (London: Pluto Press, 2000).

Rogers, Anthony. *Someone Else's War* (New York: HarperCollins, 1998).

Rubin, Elizabeth. "An Army of One's Own," *Harper's Magazine* 294 (February 1997): 44–55.

Shearer, David. *Private Armies and Military Intervention* (London: Oxford University Press, International Institute for Strategic Studies Adelphi Paper 316, 1998).

Taulbee, James Larry. "Mercenaries, Private Armies and Security Companies in Contemporary Policy," *International Politics* 37 (December 2000): 433–456.

Thomson, Janice E. *Mercenaries, Pirates, and Sovereigns: State-Building and Extraterritorial Violence in Early Modern Europe* (Princeton, NJ: Princeton University Press, 1994).

Toffler, Alvin, and Heidi Toffler. *War and Anti-War: Survival at the Dawn of the 21st Century* (Boston: Little, Brown, 1993).

Van Creveld, Martin. *The Transformation of War* (New York: The Free Press, 1991).

Zarate, Juan Carlos. "The Emergence of a New Dog of War: Private International Security Companies, International Law, and the New World Disorder," *Stanford Journal of International Law* 34 (winter 1998): 75–162.

INDEX

ABOUT THE BOOK

What does the increasing use of private security forces mean for governments? For individuals? *Armies Without States* offers a comprehensive analysis of the varieties, causes, and consequences of this growing phenomenon.

Ranging from the international to the subnational level and from the use of mercenaries by private parties to the government outsourcing of military operations, Mandel reveals emerging trends and discovers parallels among security privatization situations in all parts of the world. Brief case studies illustrate the broader themes discussed. The book concludes with an assessment of the complexities surrounding responses to security privatization—and an exploration of when, and whether, it should be promoted rather than prevented.

Robert Mandel is professor of international affairs at Lewis and Clark College. He is the author of five previous books including most recently *The Changing Face of National Security* and *Deadly Transfers and the Global Playground.*